THE HOLY SPIRIT

Who He is, What He Does, & Why You Should Care

By R.A. Torrey

Updated, Revised, and Additional Writing

By Barry L. Davis

Copyright©2013 Barry L. Davis

GodSpeed Publishing

A large portion of this work is derived from R.A. Torrey's *The Person and Work of The Holy Spirit* published in 1910 and now in the public domain. The original work has been heavily edited with modern language and Scripture Translation as well as additional studies and writings by Dr. Barry L. Davis

Visit Us for More Great Resources at:

www.amazon.com/author/barrydavis
www.pastorshelper.com

Table of Contents

CHAPTER 1: THE PERSONALITY OF THE HOLY SPIRIT

Before a person can correctly understand the work of the Holy Spirit, he must first of all know the Spirit Himself. A frequent source of error and fanaticism about the work of the Holy Spirit is the attempt to study and understand His work without first of all coming to know Him as a Person.

It is of the highest importance that we decide whether the Holy Spirit is a Divine Person, worthy to receive our adoration, our faith, our love, and our entire surrender, or whether it is simply an influence emanating from God or a power or an illumination that God imparts to us. If the Holy Spirit is a person, and a Divine Person, and we do not know Him in this way, then we are robbing a Divine Being of the worship and the faith and the love and the surrender to which He is due.

It is also of the highest importance that we decide whether the Holy Spirit is merely some mysterious and wonderful power that we in our weakness and ignorance are somehow to get hold of and use, or whether the Holy Spirit is a real Person, infinitely holy, infinitely wise, infinitely mighty and infinitely tender who is to get hold of and use us.

If we think of the Holy Spirit as merely a power or influence, our constant thought will be, "How can I get more of the Holy Spirit," but if we think of Him in the Biblical way as a Divine Person, our thought will rather be, "How can the Holy Spirit have more of me?" The conception of the Holy Spirit as a Divine influence or power that we are somehow to get hold of and use, leads to self-exaltation and self-sufficiency.

It is of the highest importance from the standpoint of experience that we know the Holy Spirit as a person. Thousands and tens of thousands of men and women can testify to the blessing that has come into their own lives as they have come to know the Holy Spirit, not merely as a gracious influence but as a real Person, just as real as Jesus Christ Himself, an ever-present, loving Friend and mighty

Helper, who is not only always by their side but dwells in their heart every day and every hour and who is ready to undertake for them in every emergency of life. Thousands of ministers, Christian workers and Christians in the humblest spheres of life can speak to the complete transformation of their Christian experience that came to them when they understood that the Holy Spirit was a Person and came to know Him.

There are at least four distinct lines of proof in the Bible that the Holy Spirit is a person.

1. *All the distinctive characteristics of personality are attributed to the Holy Spirit in the Bible.*

What are the distinctive characteristics, or marks, of personality? Knowledge, feeling or emotion, and will. Any entity that thinks and feels and wills is a person. When we say that the Holy Spirit is a person, there are those who understand us to mean that the Holy Spirit has hands and feet and eyes and ears and mouth, and so on, but these are not the characteristics of personality but of a physical body. All of these characteristics or marks of personality are repeatedly attributed to the Holy Spirit in the Old and New Testaments.

> *But God has revealed it to us by his Spirit. The Spirit searches all things, even the deep things of God. For who among men knows the thoughts of a man except the man's spirit within him? In the same way no one knows the thoughts of God except the Spirit of God.* – 1 Corinthians 2:10-11

Here knowledge is attributed to the Holy Spirit. We are clearly taught that the Holy Spirit is not merely an influence that illuminates our minds to comprehend the truth but a Being who Himself knows the truth.

> *All these are the work of one and the same Spirit, and he gives them to each one, just as he determines.* – 1 Corinthians 12:11

Here will is attributed to the Spirit and we are taught that the Holy Spirit is not a power that we get hold of and use according to our will but a Person of sovereign majesty, who uses us according to His will. This distinction is of fundamental importance in our getting into right relations with the Holy Spirit.

It is at this very point that many honest seekers after power and efficiency in service go astray. They are reaching out after and struggling to get possession of some mysterious and mighty power that they can make use of in their work according to their own will. They will never get possession of the power they seek until they come to recognize that there is not some Divine power for them to get hold of and use in their blindness and ignorance but that there is a Person, infinitely wise, as well as infinitely mighty, who is willing to take possession of them and use them according to His own perfect will.

> *And he who searches our hearts knows the mind of the Spirit, because the Spirit intercedes for the saints in accordance with God's will.* – Romans 8:27

In this passage mind is attributed to the Holy Spirit. The Greek word translated "mind" is a comprehensive word, including the ideas of thought, feeling and purpose. It is the same that is used in Romans 8:7:

> *The sinful mind is hostile to God. It does not submit to God's law, nor can it do so.* – Romans 8:7

So then in this passage we have all the distinctive marks of personality attributed to the Holy Spirit.

We find the personality of the Holy Spirit brought out in a most touching and suggestive way in Romans 15:30:

> *I urge you, brothers, by our Lord Jesus Christ and by the love of the Spirit, to join me in my struggle by praying to God for me.* – Romans 15:30

Here we have "LOVE" attributed to the Holy Spirit. We would do well to stop and consider these five words, "THE LOVE OF THE SPIRIT." We often dwell upon the love of God the Father. It is the subject of our daily and constant thought. We also often dwell upon the love of Jesus Christ the Son.

Who would think of calling himself a Christian who went a day without meditating on the love of his Savior, but how often have we meditated upon "THE LOVE OF THE SPIRIT"? Each day of our lives, if we are living as Christians should, we kneel down in the presence of God the Father and look up into His face and say, "I thank You, Father, for Your great love that led You to give Your only Son to die upon the cross of Calvary for me." Each day of our lives we also look up into the face of our Lord and Savior, Jesus Christ, and say, "Oh, glorious Lord and Savior, Jesus Son of God, I thank You for Your great love that led You to empty Yourself and forsaking all the glory of heaven, come down to earth with all its shame and to take my sins upon You and die in my place upon the cross of Calvary."

But how often do we kneel and say to the Holy Spirit, "Oh, eternal and infinite Spirit of God, I thank You for Your great love that led You to come into this world of sin and darkness and to seek me out and to follow me so patiently until You brought me to see my utter ruin and need of a Savior and to reveal to me my Lord and Savior, Jesus Christ, as just the Savior who I need."

Yet we owe our salvation just as truly to the love of the Spirit as we do to the love of the Father and the love of the Son. If it had not been for the love of God the Father looking down upon me in my utter ruin and providing a perfect atonement for me in the death of His own Son on the cross of Calvary, I would have been in hell today. If it had not been for the love of Jesus Christ, the eternal Word of God, looking upon me in my utter ruin and in obedience to the Father, putting aside all the glory of heaven for all the shame of earth and taking my place, the place of the curse, upon the cross of Calvary and pouring out His life utterly for me, I would have been in hell today. But if it had not been for the love of the Holy Spirit, sent by the Father in answer to the prayer of the Son (John 14:16) leading Him to seek me out in my utter blindness and ruin and to follow me day after day, week after week, and year after year, when I persistently turned a deaf ear to His pleadings, following me through paths of sin where it must have been agony for that holy One to go, until at last I listened and He opened my eyes to see my utter ruin and then revealed Jesus to me as just the Savior that would meet my every need and then enabled me to receive this Jesus as my own Savior; if it had not been for this patient, long-suffering, never-tiring, infinitely-tender love of the Holy Spirit, I would have been in hell today. Oh, the Holy Spirit is not merely an influence or a power or an illumination but is a Person just as real as God the Father or Jesus Christ His Son.

The personality of the Holy Spirit comes out in the Old Testament as truly as in the New:

> *You gave your good Spirit to instruct them. You did not withhold your manna from their mouths, and you gave them water for their thirst.* – Nehemiah 9:20

Here both intelligence and goodness are attributed to the Holy Spirit. There are some who tell us that while it is true the personality of the Holy Spirit is found in the New Testament, it is not found in the Old. But it is certainly found in this passage. As a matter of course, the doctrine of the personality of the Holy Spirit is not as fully developed in the Old Testament as in the New. But the doctrine is there.

There is perhaps no passage in the entire Bible in which the personality of the Holy Spirit comes out more tenderly and touchingly than in Ephesians 4:30:

> *And do not grieve the Holy Spirit of God, with whom you were sealed for the day of redemption.* – Ephesians 4:30

Here grief is attributed to the Holy Spirit. The Holy Spirit is not a blind, impersonal influence or power that comes into our lives to illuminate, sanctify and empower them. No, He is immeasurably more than that, He is a holy Person who comes to dwell in our hearts, One who sees clearly every act we perform, every word we speak, every thought we entertain, even the most fleeting desire that is allowed to pass through our minds; and if there is anything in act, or word or deed that is impure, unholy, unkind, selfish, mean, petty or untrue, this infinitely holy One is deeply grieved by it.

I know of no thought that will help you more than this to lead a holy life and to walk softly in the presence of the holy One. How often a young person is kept back from yielding to the temptations that surround them by the thought that if they would give into the temptation that now assails them, their mother might hear about it and would be grieved beyond expression. How often some young man has had his hand upon the door of some place of sin that he is about to enter and the thought has come to him, "If I do this, my mother might find out and it would nearly kill her," and so he turned his back on that door and went away to lead a pure life, so he wouldn't grieve his mother.

But there is One who is holier than any mother, One who is more sensitive against sin than the purest woman who ever walked this earth, and who loves us as even no mother ever loved, and this One dwells in our hearts, if we are really Christians, and He sees every act we do by day or under cover of the night; He hears every word we utter in public or in private; He sees every thought we entertain, He beholds every desire and imagination that is permitted even a momentary place in our mind, and if there is anything unholy, impure, selfish, mean, petty, unkind, harsh, unjust, or in anyway evil act or word or thought, He is grieved by it. If we will allow those words, "*do not grieve the Holy Spirit of God*," to sink into our hearts and become the motto of our lives, they will keep us from many sins.

2. *Many acts that only a Person can perform are attributed to the Holy Spirit.*

If we deny the personality of the Holy Spirit, many passages of Scripture become meaningless and absurd. For example, we read in 1 Corinthians 2:10:

> But God has revealed it to us by his Spirit. *The Spirit searches all things, even the deep things of God*. – 1 Corinthians 2:10

This passage sets before us the Holy Spirit, not merely as an illumination whereby we are enabled to grasp the deep things of God, but as a Person who Himself searches the deep things of God and then reveals to us the precious discoveries He has made.

"He who has an ear, let him hear what the Spirit says to the churches. To him who overcomes, I will give the right to eat from the tree of life, which is in the paradise of God." – Revelation 2:7

Here the Holy Spirit is set before us, not merely as an impersonal enlightenment that comes to our mind but a Person who speaks and out of the depths of His own wisdom, whispers into the ear of His listening servant the precious truth of God.

Because you are sons, God sent the Spirit of his Son into our hearts, the Spirit who calls out, "Abba, Father." – Galatians 4:6

Here the Holy Spirit is represented as calling out to the heart of the individual believer. Not merely a Divine influence producing in our own hearts the assurance of our sonship but one who cries out in our hearts, who bears witness together with our spirit that we are children of God. (See also Romans 8:16.)

The Holy Spirit is also represented in the Scripture as one who prays:

In the same way, the Spirit helps us in our weakness. We do not know what we ought to pray for, but the Spirit himself intercedes for us with groans that words cannot express. – Romans 8:26

It is plain from this passage that the Holy Spirit is not merely an influence that moves us to pray, not merely an illumination that teaches us how to pray, but a Person who Himself prays in and through us. There is wonderful comfort in the thought that every true believer has two Divine Persons praying for him, Jesus Christ, the Son who was once upon this earth, who knows all about our temptations, who can be touched with the feeling of our infirmities and who is now ascended to the right hand of the Father and in that place of authority and power ever lives to make intercession for us (Hebrews 7:25; 1 John 2:1); and another Person, just as Divine as He is, who walks by our side each day, who dwells in the innermost depths of our being and knows our needs, even as we do not know them ourselves, and from these depths makes intercession to the

Father for us. The position of the believer is indeed one of perfect security with these two Divine Persons praying for him.

"When the Counselor comes, whom I will send to you from the Father, the Spirit of truth who goes out from the Father, <u>he will testify about me</u>." – John 15:26

Here the Holy Spirit is set before us as a Person who gives His testimony to Jesus Christ, not merely as an illumination that enables the believer to testify of Christ, but a Person who Himself testifies; and a clear distinction is drawn in this and the following verse between the testimony of the Holy Spirit and the testimony of the believer to whom He bears witness, for we read in the next verse:

"And <u>you also</u> must testify, for you have been with me from the beginning." – John 15:27

So there are two witnesses, the Holy Spirit bearing witness to the believer and the believer bearing witness to the world.

The Holy Spirit is also spoken of as a teacher.

But the Counselor, the Holy Spirit, whom the Father will send in my name, will teach you all things and will remind you of everything I have said to you. – John 14:26

And in a similar way, we read in John 16:12-14:

"I have much more to say to you, more than you can now bear. But when he, the Spirit of truth, comes, <u>he will guide you into all truth</u>. He will not speak on his own; he will speak only what he hears, and he will tell you what is yet to come. He will bring glory to me by taking from what is mine and making it known to you." – John 16:12-14

And in the Old Testament, Nehemiah 9:20:

You gave your good Spirit to instruct them. – Nehemiah 9:20a

In all these passages it is perfectly clear that the Holy Spirit is not a mere illumination that enables us to apprehend the truth, but a Person who comes to us to teach us day by day the truth of God. It is the privilege of the most humble believer in Jesus Christ not merely to have his mind illuminated to comprehend the truth of God, but to have a Divine Teacher to daily teach him the truth he needs to know (1 John 2:20, 27).

The Holy Spirit is also represented as the Leader and Guide of the children of God:

> *Because those who are led by the Spirit of God are sons of God.* – Romans 8:14

He is not merely an influence that enables us to see the way that God would have us go, nor merely a power that gives us strength to go that way, but a Person who takes us by the hand and gently leads us on in the paths in which God would have us walk.

The Holy Spirit is also represented as a Person who has authority to command men in their service of Jesus Christ. We read of the Apostle Paul and his companions in Acts 16:6-7:

> *Paul and his companions traveled throughout the region of Phrygia and Galatia, having been kept by the Holy Spirit from preaching the word in the province of Asia. When they came to the border of Mysia, they tried to enter Bithynia, but the Spirit of Jesus would not allow them to.* – Acts 16:6-7

Here it is a Person who takes the direction of the conduct of Paul and his companions and a Person whose authority they recognized and to whom they instantly submit.

Further still than this the Holy Spirit is represented as the One who is the supreme authority in the church, who calls men to work and appoints them to office:

> *While they were worshiping the Lord and fasting, the Holy Spirit said, "Set apart for me Barnabas and Saul for the work to which I have called them."* – Acts 13:2

> *Keep watch over yourselves and all the flock of which the Holy Spirit has made you overseers. Be shepherds of the church of God, which he bought with his own blood.* – Acts 20:28

There can be no doubt to a candid seeker after truth that it is a Person, and a person of Divine majesty and sovereignty, who is set here before us.

From all the passages quoted, it is evident that many acts that only a person can perform are attributed to the Holy Spirit.

3. A designation is given for the Holy Spirit that can only be designated to a person.

> "And I will ask the Father, and he will give you another Counselor to be with you forever-- the Spirit of truth. The world cannot accept him, because it neither sees him nor knows him. But you know him, for he lives with you and will be in you." – John 14:16-17

Our Lord had announced to the disciples that He was about to leave them. An awful sense of desolation took possession of them. Sorrow filled their hearts (John 16:6) at the contemplation of their loneliness and absolute helplessness when Jesus would leave them alone. To comfort them the Lord tells them that they will not be left alone, but that in leaving them He was going to the Father and that He would pray to the Father and He would give them another Counselor to take the place of Himself during His absence.

Is it possible that Jesus Christ could have used such language if the other Counselor who was coming to take His place was only an impersonal influence or power? Still more, is it possible that Jesus could have said as He did in John 16:7:

> "But I tell you the truth: It is for your good that I am going away. Unless I go away, the Counselor will not come to you; but if I go, I will send him to you." – John 16:7

If this Counselor whom He was to send was simply an impersonal influence or power? No, one Divine Person was going, another Person just as Divine Person was coming to take His place, and it was expedient for the disciples that the One go to represent them before the Father, for another just as Divine and sufficient was coming to take His place. This promise of our Lord and Savior of the coming of the other Counselor and of His abiding with us is the greatest and best of all for the present age. This is THE promise of the Father (Acts 1:4), the promise of promises. We will look into this further when we study the names of the Holy Spirit.

4. *Actions are directed toward the Holy Spirit that could only be directed to a Person.*

Yet they rebelled and grieved his Holy Spirit. So he turned and became their enemy and he himself fought against them. – Isaiah 63:10

Here we are told that the Holy Spirit is rebelled against and grieved (Ephesians 4:30). Only a person can be rebelled against and only a person of authority. Only a person can be grieved. You cannot grieve a mere influence or power.

How much more severely do you think a man deserves to be punished who has trampled the Son of God under foot, who has treated as an unholy thing the blood of the covenant that sanctified him, and who has insulted the Spirit of grace? – Hebrews 10:29

Here we are told that the Holy Spirit was "insulted." There is only one kind of entity in the universe that can be insulted and that is a person. It is absurd to think of insulting an influence or a power or any kind of being except a person.

Then Peter said, "Ananias, how is it that Satan has so filled your heart that you have lied to the Holy Spirit and have kept for yourself some of the money you received for the land?" – Acts 5:3

Here we have the Holy Spirit represented as one who can be lied to. One cannot lie to anything but a person.

"And so I tell you, every sin and blasphemy will be forgiven men, but the blasphemy against the Spirit will not be forgiven. Anyone who speaks a word against the Son of Man will be forgiven, but anyone who speaks against the Holy Spirit will not be forgiven, either in this age or in the age to come." – Matthew 12:31-32

Here we are told that the Holy Spirit is blasphemed against. It is impossible to blaspheme anything but a person. If the Holy Spirit is not a person, it certainly cannot be a more serious and decisive sin to blaspheme Him than it is to blaspheme the Son of man, our Lord and Savior, Jesus Christ Himself.

Here then we have four distinctive and decisive lines of proof THAT THE HOLY SPIRIT IS A PERSON. Theoretically most of us believe this but do we, in our real thought of Him and in our practical attitude towards Him treat Him as if He were indeed a Person?

If most Christians were questioned in regard to what they believe, they would say that they believed that there were three Persons in the Godhead, Father, Son and Holy Spirit. But a theological confession is one thing, a practical realization of the truth we confess is quite another.

Do you regard the Holy Spirit as real a Person as Jesus Christ, as loving and wise and strong, as worthy of your confidence and love and surrender as Jesus Christ Himself?

The Holy Spirit came into this world to be to the disciples of our Lord after His departure, and to us, what Jesus Christ had been to them during the days of His personal companionship with them (John 14:16-17). Is He that to you? Do you know Him?

Here lies the whole secret of a real Christian life, a life of liberty and joy and power and fullness. To have as your ever-present Friend, and to be conscious that you have as your ever-present Friend, the Holy Spirit, and to surrender your life entirely to His control – this is true Christian living.

The doctrine of the Personality of the Holy Spirit is as distinctive of Christianity as the doctrines of the Deity and the atonement of Jesus Christ Himself. But it is not enough to believe the doctrine—you must know the Holy Spirit Himself. The whole purpose of this lesson (God help me to say it reverently) was to introduce you to my Friend, the Holy Spirit.

CHAPTER 2: THE DEITY OF THE HOLY SPIRIT

In the preceding chapter we saw clearly that the Holy Spirit is a Person. But what sort of a Person is He? Is He a finite person or an infinite person? Is He God? This question also is plainly answered in the Bible. There are in the Scriptures of the Old and New Testaments five distinct and decisive lines of proof of the Deity of the Holy Spirit.

World English Dictionary

deity

— *n* , *pl* **-ties**

1. a god or goddess

2. the state of being divine; godhead

3. the rank, status, or position of a god

4. the nature or character of God

---

1. *Each of the four distinctively Divine attributes is attributed to the Holy Spirit.*

What are the distinctively Divine attributes? Eternity, omnipresence (in all places at all times), omniscience (possesses all knowledge) and omnipotence (all powerful). All of these are attributed to the Holy Spirit in the Bible.

We find ETERNITY attributed to the Holy Spirit in Hebrews 9:14:

How much more, then, will the blood of Christ, who through the eternal Spirit offered himself unblemished to God, cleanse our consciences from acts that lead to death, so that we may serve the living God! – Hebrews 9:14

OMNIPRESENCE is attributed to the Holy Spirit in Psalm 139:7-10:

Where can I go from your Spirit? Where can I flee from your presence? If I go up to the heavens, you are there; if I make my bed in the depths, you are there. If I rise on the wings of the dawn, if I settle on the far side of the sea, even there your hand will guide me, your right hand will hold me fast. – Psalms 139:7-10

OMNISCIENCE is attributed to the Holy Spirit in several passages:

But God has revealed it to us by his Spirit. The Spirit searches all things, even the deep things of God. For who among men knows the thoughts of a man except the man's spirit within him? In the same way no one knows the thoughts of God except the Spirit of God. – 1 Corinthians 2:10-11

"But the Counselor, the Holy Spirit, whom the Father will send in my name, will <u>teach you all things</u> and will remind you of everything I have said to you." – John 14:26

"I have much more to say to you, more than you can now bear. But when he, the Spirit of truth, comes, <u>he will guide you into all truth</u>. He will not speak on his own; he will speak only what he hears, and he will tell you what is yet to come." – John 16:12-13

We find OMNIPOTENCE attributed to the Holy Spirit in Luke 1:35:

The angel answered, "The Holy Spirit will come upon you, and <u>the power of the Most High</u> will overshadow you. So the holy one to be born will be called the Son of God." – Luke 1:35

2. Three distinctively Divine works are attributed to the Holy Spirit.

When we think of God and His work, the first work that we always think is creation. In the Scriptures creation is attributed to the Holy Spirit:

The Spirit of God <u>has made me</u>; the breath of the Almighty gives me life. – Job 33:4

When you send your Spirit, <u>they are created</u>, and you renew the face of the earth. – Psalms 104:30

In connection with the description of creation in the first chapter of Genesis, the activity of the Spirit is referred to (Genesis 1:1-3).

The impartation of life is also a Divine work and this is attributed in the Scriptures to the Holy Spirit:

"The Spirit gives life; the flesh counts for nothing." – John 6:63a
And if the Spirit of him who raised Jesus from the dead is living in you, he who raised Christ from the dead will also give life to your mortal bodies <u>through his Spirit</u>, who lives in you. – Romans 8:11

In the description of the creation of man in Genesis 2:7, it is the breath of God, that is the Holy Spirit, who imparts life to man, and man becomes a living soul:

The LORD God formed the man from the dust of the ground and breathed into his nostrils <u>the breath of life</u>, and the man became a living being. – Genesis 2:7

The Greek word which is rendered "breath" is translated "spirit" in other translations. And though the Holy Spirit as a Person does not come out distinctly in this early reference to Him in Genesis 2:7, nevertheless, this passage interpreted in the light of the fuller revelation of the New Testament clearly refers to the Holy Spirit.

The authorship of Divine prophecies is also attributed to the Holy Spirit:

For prophecy never had its origin in the will of man, but men spoke from God as <u>they were carried along by the Holy Spirit</u>. – 2 Peter 1:21

Even in the Old Testament, there is a reference to the Holy Spirit as the author of prophecy. We read in 2 Samuel 23:2-3:

"The Spirit of the LORD spoke through me; his word was on my tongue. The God of Israel spoke, the Rock of Israel said to me: 'When one rules over men in righteousness, when he rules in the fear of God...'" – 2 Samuel 23:2-3

So we see that the three distinctly Divine works of creation, the impartation of life, and prophecy are attributed to the Holy Spirit.

3. Statements in the Old Testament that specifically name the LORD (or Yahweh) as their subject are applied to the Holy Spirit in the New Testament.

A striking illustration of this is found in Isaiah 6:8-10:

Then I heard the voice of the LORD saying, "Whom shall I send? And who will go for us?" And I said, "Here am I. Send me!" He said, "Go and tell this people: "'Be ever hearing, but never understanding; be ever seeing, but never perceiving.' Make the heart of this people calloused; make their ears dull and close their eyes. Otherwise they might see with their eyes, hear with their ears, understand with their hearts, and turn and be healed." – Isaiah 6:8-10

In verse five we are told that it was Yahweh (note: whenever the word LORD is spelled in capitals in the Old Testament, it stands for Yahweh in the Hebrew) whom Isaiah saw and who speaks. But in Acts 28:25-27 there is a reference to this statement of Isaiah's and where in Isaiah we are told it is Yahweh who speaks, in the reference in Acts we are told that it was the Holy Spirit who was the speaker:

They disagreed among themselves and began to leave after Paul had made this final statement: "The Holy Spirit spoke the truth to your forefathers when he said through Isaiah the prophet: "'Go to this people and say, "You will be ever hearing but never understanding; you will be ever seeing but never perceiving." For this people's heart has become calloused; they hardly hear with their ears, and they have closed their eyes. Otherwise they might see with their eyes, hear with their ears, understand with their hearts and turn, and I would heal them.' – Acts 28:25-27

So we see that what is distinctly attributed to Yahweh in the Old Testament is attributed to the Holy Spirit in the New: *i. e.*, the Holy Spirit is identified with Yahweh. It is a noteworthy fact that in John 12:39-41 where another reference is made to this passage in Isaiah, this same passage is attributed to Christ (note carefully the forty-first verse). So in different parts of Scripture, we have the same passage referred to Yahweh, referred to the Holy Spirit, and referred to Jesus Christ. May we not find the explanation of this in the threefold "Holy" of the seraphim in Isaiah 6:3, where we read:

And they were calling to one another: "Holy, holy, holy is the LORD Almighty; the whole earth is full of his glory." – Isaiah 6:3

In this we have a distinct suggestion of the tri-personality of the Yahweh of Hosts, and therefore, the propriety of the threefold application of the vision. A further suggestion of this tri-personality of Yahweh of Hosts is found in the eighth verse of the chapter where the Lord is represented as saying:

Then I heard the voice of the Lord saying, "Whom shall I send? And who will go for us?" – Isaiah 6:8

Another striking illustration of the application of passages in the New Testament to the Holy Spirit which in the Old Testament distinctly name Yahweh as their subject is found in Exodus 16:7:

"And in the morning you will see the glory of the LORD, because he has heard your grumbling against him. Who are we, that you should grumble against us?" – Exodus 16:7

Here the grumbling of the children of Israel is distinctly said to be against Yahweh. But in Hebrews 3:7-9, where this instance is referred to, we read:

So, as the Holy Spirit says: "Today, if you hear his voice, do not harden your hearts as you did in the rebellion, during the time of testing in the desert, where your fathers tested and tried me and for forty years saw what I did." – Hebrews 3:7-9

The grumblings which Moses in the Book of Exodus says were against Yahweh, we are told in the Epistle to the Hebrews were against the Holy Spirit. This leaves it beyond question that the Holy

Spirit occupies the position of Yahweh (or Deity) in the New Testament.

4. *The name of the Holy Spirit is joined with the name of God in a way that demonstrates their relationship and equality.*

We have an illustration of this in 1 Corinthians 12:4-6:

> *There are different kinds of gifts, but the <u>same</u> Spirit. There are different kinds of service, but the <u>same</u> Lord. There are different kinds of working, but the <u>same</u> God works all of them in all men.* – 1 Corinthians 12:4-6

Here we find God, and the Lord and the Spirit associated together in a relation of equality that would be shocking to contemplate if the Spirit were a finite being. We have a still more striking illustration of this in Matthew 28:19:

> *"Therefore go and make disciples of all nations, baptizing them in the name of the <u>Father</u> and of the <u>Son</u> and of the <u>Holy Spirit</u>."* – Matthew 28:19

Could anyone, who had grasped the Bible conception of God the Father, think for a moment of adding the name of the Holy Spirit in this way if the Holy Spirit were a finite being, even the most exalted of angelic beings?

Another striking illustration is found in 2 Corinthians 13:14:

> *May the grace of the <u>Lord Jesus Christ</u>, and the love of <u>God</u>, and the fellowship of the <u>Holy Spirit</u> be with you all.* – 2 Corinthians 13:14

Can any one ponder these words and catch anything like their real import without seeing clearly that it would be impossible to join the name of the Holy Spirit with that of God the Father in the way in which it is joined in this verse except for the fact that the Holy Spirit were Himself a Divine Being?

5. *The Holy Spirit is called God.*

The final and decisive proof of the Deity of the Holy Spirit is found in the fact that He is called God in the New Testament:

> *Then Peter said, "Ananias, how is it that Satan has so filled your heart that you have lied to the Holy Spirit and have kept for yourself some of the money you received for the land? Didn't it belong to you before it was sold? And after it was sold, wasn't the money at your disposal? What made you think of doing such a thing? You have not lied to men but to God." –* Acts 5:3-4

In the first part of this passage we are told that Ananias lied to the Holy Spirit. Yet, when this is further explained, we are told that it was not to men but to God that he had lied to. In other words, the Holy Spirit to whom he lied is called God.

To sum it all up, by the recognition of all the distinctively Divine attributes, and several distinctly Divine works, by referring statements which in the Old Testament clearly name Yahweh, the Lord, or God as their subject to the Holy Spirit in the New Testament, by joining the name of the Holy Spirit with that of God in a way that would be impossible to join that of any finite being with that of Deity, by plainly calling the Holy Spirit God, in all these unmistakable ways, God in His own Word distinctly proclaims that the Holy Spirit is a Divine Person.

CHAPTER 3: THE DISTINCTIVE ROLE OF THE HOLY SPIRIT IN THE TRINITY

1. *Distinctive Role.*

We have seen so far that the Holy Spirit is a Person and a Divine Person. And now another question arises – Is He as a Person separate and distinct from the Father and from the Son? A person who carefully studies the New Testament statements cannot help but discover that beyond any doubt He is.

> *When all the people were being baptized, Jesus was baptized too. And as he was praying, heaven was opened and the Holy Spirit descended on him in bodily form like a dove. And a voice came from heaven: "You are my Son, whom I love; with you I am well pleased."* – Luke 3:21-22

Here the clearest possible distinction is drawn between Jesus Christ, who was on earth, and the Father who spoke to Him from heaven as one person speaks to another person, and the Holy Spirit who descended in a bodily form as a dove from the Father, and rested upon the Son as a Person separate and distinct from Himself.

We see a clear distinction drawn between the name of the Father and that of the Son and that of the Holy Spirit in Matthew 28:19:

> *"Therefore go and make disciples of all nations, baptizing them in the name of the Father and of the Son and of the Holy Spirit."* – Matthew 28:19

The distinction of the Holy Spirit from the Father and the Son comes out again with exceeding clearness in John 14:16:

> *"And I will ask the Father, and he will give you another Counselor to be with you forever."* – John 14:16

Here we see the one Person, the Son, praying to another Person, the Father, and the Father to whom He prays giving another Person, another Counselor, in answer to the prayer of the second Person, the Son. If words mean anything, and certainly in the Bible they mean what they say, there can be no mistaking it, that the Father and the Son and the Spirit are three distinct and separate Persons.

Again in John 16:7, a clear distinction is drawn between Jesus who goes away to the Father and the Holy Spirit who comes from the Father to take His place:

> *"But I tell you the truth: It is for your good that I am going away. Unless I go away, the Counselor will not come to you; but if I go, I will send him to you." –* John 16:7

A similar distinction is drawn in Acts 2:33, where we read:

> *Exalted to the right hand of God, he has received from the Father the promised Holy Spirit and has poured out what you now see and hear. –* Acts 2:33

In this passage, the clearest possible distinction is drawn between the Son exalted to the right hand of the Father and the Father to whose right hand He is exalted, and the Holy Spirit whom the Son receives from the Father and pours out upon the Church.

To sum it all up, again and again the Bible draws the clearest possible distinction between the three Persons, the Holy Spirit, the Father and the Son. They are three separate personalities, having mutual relations to one another, acting upon one another, speaking of or to one another, applying the pronouns of the second and third persons to one another.

2. Subordinate Role.

From the fact that the Holy Spirit is a Divine Person, it does not follow that the Holy Spirit is in every sense equal to the Father. While the Scriptures teach that in Jesus Christ dwelt all the fullness of the Godhead in a bodily form (Colossians 2:9) and that He was so truly and FULLY Divine that He could say, "I and the Father are one" (John 10:30) and "Anyone who has seen me has seen the Father" (John 14:9), they also teach with equal clearness that Jesus

Christ was not equal to the Father in every respect, but subordinate to the Father in many ways. They are all fully and completely God, yet their roles call for subordination in some respects.

The Scriptures teach us that though the Holy Spirit is a Divine Person (God), He is subordinate to the Father and to the Son:

"But the Counselor, the Holy Spirit, <u>whom the Father will send</u> in my name, will teach you all things and will remind you of everything I have said to you." – John 14:26

In this passage (John 14:26) we are taught that the Holy Spirit is sent by the Father and in the name of the Son.

In John 15:26 we are told that it is Jesus who sends the Spirit from the Father:

"When the Counselor comes, <u>whom I will send to you</u> from the Father, the Spirit of truth who goes out from the Father, he will testify about me." – John 15:26

Just as we are elsewhere taught that Jesus Christ was sent by the Father (John 6:29; 8:29, 42), we are here taught that the Holy Spirit in turn is sent by Jesus Christ.

The subordination of the Holy Spirit to the Father and the Son comes out also in the fact that He derives some of His names from the Father and from the Son:

You, however, are controlled not by the sinful nature but by the Spirit, if the <u>Spirit of God</u> lives in you. And if anyone does not have the <u>Spirit of Christ</u>, he does not belong to Christ. – Romans 8:9

Here we have two names of the Spirit, one derived from His relation to the Father, "the Spirit of God," and the other derived from His relation to the Son, "the Spirit of Christ."

In Acts 16:7, He is spoken of as "the Spirit of Jesus."

The subordination of the Spirit to the Son is also seen in the fact that the Holy Spirit, *"will not speak on his own; he will speak only what he hears."*

> *"But when he, the Spirit of truth, comes, he will guide you into all truth. He will not speak on his own; he will speak only what he hears, and he will tell you what is yet to come."* – John 16:13

In a similar way, Jesus said of Himself, *"My teaching is not my own. It comes from him who sent me"* (John 7:16; 8:26, 40).

The subordination of the Spirit to the Son comes out again in the clearly revealed fact that it is the work of the Holy Spirit not to glorify Himself but to glorify Christ.

> *"He (the Spirit) will bring glory to me by taking from what is mine and making it known to you."* – John 16:13-14

In a similar way, Christ sought not His own glory, but the glory of Him that sent Him, that is the Father (John 7:18).

From all these passages, it is evident that the Holy Spirit in His present work, while possessed of all the attributes of Deity, is subordinated to the Father and to the Son. On the other hand, we shall see later that in His earthly life, Jesus lived and taught and worked in the power of the Holy Spirit.

CHAPTER 4: THE PERSON AND WORK OF THE HOLY SPIRIT AS REVEALED IN HIS NAMES

At least twenty-two different names are used in the Old and New Testaments in speaking of the Holy Spirit. There is the deepest significance in these names. By the careful study of them, we find a wonderful revelation of the Person and work of the Holy Spirit.

1. *The Spirit.*

The simplest name by which the Holy Spirit is mentioned in the Bible is simply—"THE SPIRIT." This name is also used as the basis of other names, so we begin our study with this. The Greek and Hebrew words translated *Spirit* literally mean, "Breath" or "Wind." Both thoughts are in the name as applied to the Holy Spirit.

　　1) The Spirit as "Breath."

And with that he breathed on them and said, "Receive the Holy Spirit." – John 20:22

The LORD God formed the man from the dust of the ground and breathed into his nostrils the breath of life, and the man became a living being. – Genesis 2:7

The Spirit of God has made me; the breath of the Almighty gives me life. – Job 33:4

What is the significance of this name from the standpoint of these passages? It is that the Spirit is the outbreathing of God, His inmost life going forth in a personal form to bring us to life. When we receive the Holy Spirit, we receive the inmost life of God Himself to dwell in a personal way in us. When we really grasp this thought, it should overwhelm us. Just stop and think what it means to have the inmost life of that infinite and eternal Being whom we call God, dwelling in a personal way in you. How solemn and how wonderful and yet unspeakably glorious life becomes when we realize this.

2) The Spirit as "the Wind."

"Flesh gives birth to flesh, but the Spirit gives birth to spirit. You should not be surprised at my saying, 'You must be born again.' The wind blows wherever it pleases. You hear its sound, but you cannot tell where it comes from or where it is going. So it is with everyone born of the Spirit." – John 3:6-8

In the Greek, it is the same word that is translated in one part of this passage "Spirit" and the other part of the passage "wind." And it would seem as if the word ought to be translated the same way in both parts of the passage. It would then read, *"Flesh gives birth to flesh, but the Wind gives birth to wind. You should not be surprised at my saying, 'You must be born again.' The wind blows wherever it pleases. You hear its sound, but you cannot tell where it comes from or where it is going. So it is with everyone born of the Wind."*

The full significance of this name as applied to the Holy Spirit (or Holy Wind) it may be beyond us to fathom, but we can see at least this much of its meaning:

(1) The Spirit like the wind is SOVEREIGN.

"The wind blows wherever it pleases" (John 3:8). You cannot dictate to the wind. It does as it wills. The same is true of the Holy Spirit—He is sovereign—we cannot dictate to Him. When the wind is blowing from the north you may long to have it blow from the south, but cry as loudly as you like to the wind, "Blow from the south" and it will keep right on blowing from the north. But while you cannot dictate to the wind, while it blows as it will, you may learn the laws that govern the wind's motions and by bringing yourself into harmony with those laws, you can get the wind to do your work. You can erect your windmill so that whichever way the wind blows from the wheels will turn and the wind will grind your grain, or pump your water. Just so, while we cannot dictate to the Holy Spirit we can learn the laws of His operations and by bringing ourselves into harmony with those laws, above all by submitting our wills absolutely to His sovereign will, the sovereign Spirit of God will work through us and accomplish His own glorious work by our participation.

(2) The Spirit like the wind is INVISIBLE BUT NONE THE LESS PERCEPTIBLE AND REAL AND MIGHTY.

You hear the sound of the wind (John 3:8) but the wind itself you never see. You hear the voice of the Spirit but He Himself is always invisible. (The word translated "sound" in John 3:8 is the word which elsewhere is translated "voice.") We not only hear the voice of the wind but we see its mighty effects. We feel the breath of the wind upon our cheeks, we see the dust and the leaves blowing before the wind, we see the vessels at sea driven swiftly towards their ports; but the wind itself remains invisible. The same is true with the Spirit; we feel His breath upon our souls, we see the mighty things He does, but Himself we do not see. He is invisible, but He is real and perceptible. None of us have seen the Holy Spirit at any time, but of His presence we have been distinctly conscious again and again and again. His mighty power we have witnessed and His reality we cannot doubt. There are those who tell us that they do not believe in anything which they cannot see. Not one of them has ever seen the wind but they all believe in the wind. They have felt the wind and they have seen its effects, and similarly we, beyond any question, have felt the mighty presence of the Spirit and witnessed His mighty workings.

(3) The Spirit like the wind is MYSTERIOUS.

"You cannot tell where it comes from or where it is going." Nothing in nature is more mysterious than the wind. But more mysterious still is the Holy Spirit in His operations. We hear of how suddenly and unexpectedly in widely separated communities He begins to do His mighty work. Doubtless there are hidden reasons why He does His work in this way, but often-times these reasons are completely undiscoverable by us. We do not know where He comes from or where He is going. We cannot tell where the next place might be that He will display His mighty and gracious power.

(4) The Spirit, like the wind, is INDISPENSABLE.

Jesus answered, "I tell you the truth, no one can enter the kingdom of God unless he is born of water and the Spirit." – John 3:5

If the wind should absolutely cease to blow for a single hour, most of the life on this earth would cease to be. Time and again when the health reports of the different cities of the United States are issued, it has been found that the five healthiest cities in the United States were five cities located on the great lakes. Many have been surprised at this report when they have visited some of these cities and found that they were far from being the cleanest cities, or the most sanitary, and yet year after year this report has been returned. The explanation is simply this, it is the wind blowing from the lakes that has brought life and health to the cities. When the Spirit ceases to blow in any heart or any church or any community, death ensues, but when the Spirit blows steadily upon the individual or the church or the community, there is abounding spiritual life and health.

(5) The Spirit, like the wind, is LIFE GIVING.

"The Spirit gives life; the flesh counts for nothing. The words I have spoken to you are spirit and they are life." – John 6:63

He has made us competent as ministers of a new covenant--not of the letter but of the Spirit; for the letter kills, but the Spirit gives life. – 2 Corinthians 3:6

Perhaps the most suggestive passage on this point is Ezekiel 37:8-10:

I looked, and tendons and flesh appeared on them and skin covered them, but there was no breath in them. Then he said to me, "Prophesy to the breath; prophesy, son of man, and say to it, 'This is what the Sovereign LORD says: Come from the four winds, O breath, and breathe into these slain, that they may live.'" So I prophesied as he commanded me, and breath entered them; they came to life and stood up on their feet--a vast army. – Ezekiel 37:8-10

Israel, in the prophet's vision, was only bones, very many and very dry (vv. 2, 11), until the prophet proclaimed unto them the word of God; then there was a noise and a shaking and the bones came together, bone to his bone, and the sinews and the flesh came upon the bones, but still there was no life, but when the wind blew, the breath of God's Spirit, then *"they came to life and stood up on their feet – a vast army."* All life in the individual believer, in the teacher, the preacher, and the church is the Holy Spirit's work.

You will sometimes make the acquaintance of a man, and as you hear him talk and observe his conduct, you are repelled and disgusted. Everything about him declares that he is a dead man, a moral corpse and not only dead but rapidly putrefying. You get away from him as quickly as you can. Months afterwards you meet him again. You hesitate to speak to him; you want to get out of his very presence, but you do speak to him, and he has not uttered many sentences before you notice a marvellous change. His conversation is sweet and wholesome and uplifting; everything about his manner is attractive and delightful. You soon discover that the man's whole conduct and life has been transformed. He is no longer a putrefying corpse but a living child of God. What has happened? The Wind of God has blown upon him; he has received the Holy Spirit, the Holy Wind. Some quiet day of worship you visit a church. Everything about the outward appearance of the church are all that could be desired. There is an attractive auditorium, expensive instruments, gifted vocalists, an interesting preacher. The service is well arranged but you have not been there long before you are forced to see that there is no life, that it is all form, and that there is nothing really being accomplished for God or for man. You go away with a heavy heart. Months afterwards you have the opportunity to visit the church again; the outward appearance of the church is the same as it was before but the service has not gone on long before you notice a great difference. There is a new power in the singing, a new spirit in the prayer, a new grip in the preaching, everything about the church is teeming with the life of God. What has happened? The Wind of God has blown upon that church; the Holy Spirit, the Holy Wind, has come. You go some day to hear a preacher who you have heard great things about. As he stands up to preach you soon learn that no one exaggerated when they praised his abilities from the merely intellectual and rhetorical standpoint. His diction is faultless, his style beautiful, his logic unimpeachable, his orthodoxy beyond criticism. It is an intellectual treat to listen to him, and yet after all as he preaches you cannot avoid a feeling of sadness, for there is no real grip, no real power, indeed no reality of any kind, in the man's preaching. You go away with a heavy heart at the thought of this waste of magnificent abilities. Months, perhaps years, pass by and you again find yourself listening to this celebrated preacher, but what a change! The same faultless diction, the same beautiful style, the same unimpeachable logic, the same skillful delivery, the same sound orthodoxy, but now there is something more, there is reality, life, grip, power in the preaching. Men and women sit breathless as he speaks, sinners bowed with tears of contrition, pricked to their hearts with conviction of sin; men and women and boys and girls renounce their selfishness, and their sin and their worldliness and accept Jesus Christ and surrender their lives to Him. What has happened? The Wind of God has blown upon that man. He has been filled with the Holy Wind.

(6) Like the wind, the Holy Spirit is IRRESISTIBLE.

"But you will receive power when the Holy Spirit comes on you; and you will be my witnesses in Jerusalem, and in all Judea and Samaria, and to the ends of the earth." – Acts 1:8

When this promise of our Lord was fulfilled in Stephen, we read:

But they could not stand up against his wisdom or the Spirit by whom he spoke. – Acts 6:10

A man filled with the Holy Spirit is transformed into a cyclone. What can stand before the wind? When St. Cloud, Minnesota, was visited with a cyclone years ago, the wind picked up loaded freight cars and carried them away off the track. It wrenched an iron bridge from its foundations, twisted it together and hurled it away. When a cyclone later visited St. Louis, Missouri, it cut off telegraph poles a foot in diameter as if they had been pipe stems. It cut off enormous trees close to the root, it cut off the corner of brick buildings where it passed as though they had been cut by a knife; nothing could stand before it; and so, nothing can stand before a Spirit-filled preacher of the Word. None can resist the wisdom and the Spirit by which he speaks. The Wind of God took possession of Charles G. Finney, an obscure country lawyer, and sent him through New York State, then through New England, then through England, mowing down strong men by his resistless, Spirit-given logic. One night in Rochester, scores of lawyers, led by the justice of the Court of Appeals, filed out of the pews and bowed in the aisles and yielded their lives to God. The Wind of God took possession of D. L. Moody, an uneducated young business man in Chicago, and in the power of this resistless Wind, men and women and young people were mowed down before his words and brought in humble confession and renunciation of sin to the feet of Jesus Christ, and filled with the life of God they have been the pillars in the churches of Great Britain and throughout the world ever since. The great need today in individuals, in churches and in preachers is that the Wind of God blow upon us.

2. *The Spirit of God.*

The Holy Spirit is frequently spoken of in the Bible as the Spirit of God. For example we read in 1 Corinthians 3:16:

> *Don't you know that you yourselves are God's temple and that God's Spirit lives in you?* – 1 Corinthians 3:16

In this name we have the same essential thought as in the former name, but with this addition, that His Divine origin, nature and power are emphasized. He is not merely "The Wind" as seen above, but "The Wind OF GOD."

3. *The Spirit of Yahweh.*

> *The Spirit of the LORD (Yahweh) will rest on him--the Spirit of wisdom and of understanding, the Spirit of counsel and of power, the Spirit of knowledge and of the fear of the LORD.* – Isaiah 11:2

The thought of the name is, of course, essentially the same as the preceding with the exception that God is here thought of as the Covenant God of Israel. He is spoken of in the connection in which the name is found; and, of course, the Bible, following that unerring accuracy that it always exhibits in its use of the different names for God, in this connection speaks of the Spirit as the Spirit of Yahweh and not merely as the Spirit of God.

4. *The Spirit of the Lord Yahweh.*

> *The Spirit of the Sovereign LORD (Lord Yahweh) is on me, because the LORD has anointed me to preach good news to the poor. He has sent me to bind up the brokenhearted, to proclaim freedom for the captives and release from darkness for the prisoners.* – Isaiah 61:1

The Holy Spirit is here spoken of, not merely as the Spirit of Yahweh, but the Spirit of the Lord Yahweh because of the relation in which God Himself is spoken of in this connection, as not merely Yahweh, the covenant God of Israel, but as Yahweh Israel's Lord as well as their covenant-keeping God. This name of the Spirit is even more expressive than the name "The Spirit of God."

5. *The Spirit of the Living God.*

> *You show that you are a letter from Christ, the result of our ministry, written not with ink but with the Spirit of the living God, not on tablets of stone but on tablets of human hearts.* – 2 Corinthians 3:3

What is the significance of this name? It is made clear by the context. The Apostle Paul is drawing a contrast between the Word of God written with ink on parchment and the Word of God written on *"tablets of human hearts"* by the Holy Spirit, who in this connection is called "the Spirit of the living God," because He makes God a living reality in our personal experience instead of a mere intellectual concept.

There are many who believe in God, and who are perfectly orthodox in their conception of God, but God is to them only an intellectual theological proposition. It is the work of the Holy Spirit to make God something vastly more than a theological notion, no matter how orthodox; He is the Spirit OF THE LIVING GOD, and it is His work to make God a living God to us, a Being whom we know, with whom we have personal acquaintance, a Being more real to us than the most intimate human friend we have. Have you a real God? Well, you may have. The Holy Spirit is the Spirit of the living God, and He is able and ready to give to you a living God, to make God real in your personal experience.

There are many who have a God who once lived and acted and spoke, a God who lived and acted at the creation of the universe, who perhaps lived and acted in the days of Moses and Elijah and Jesus Christ and the Apostles, but who no longer lives and acts. If He exists at all, He has withdrawn Himself from any active part in nature or the history of man. He created nature and gave it its laws and powers and now leaves it to run itself. He created man and endowed him with his various faculties but has now left him to work out his own destiny. They may go further than this: they may believe in a God, who spoke to Abraham and to Moses and to David and to Isaiah and to Jesus and to the Apostles, but who speaks no longer. We may read in the Bible what He spoke to these various men but we cannot expect Him to speak to us. In contrast with these, it is the work of the Holy Spirit, the Spirit OF THE LIVING GOD, to give us to know a God who lives and acts and speaks today, a God who is ready to come as near to us as He came to Abraham, to Moses or to Isaiah, or to the Apostles or to Jesus Himself. Not that He has any new revelations to make, for He guided the Apostles into all the truth (John 16:13): but though there has been a complete revelation of God's truth made in the Bible, still God lives today and will speak to us as directly as He spoke to His chosen ones of old. Happy is the man who knows the Holy Spirit as the Spirit of the living God, and who, consequently, has a real God, a God who lives today, a God upon whom he can depend today to work for him, a God with whom he enjoys intimate personal fellowship, a God to whom he may raise his voice in prayer and who speaks back to him.

6. *The Spirit of Christ.*

> *You, however, are controlled not by the sinful nature but by the Spirit, if the Spirit of God lives in you. And if anyone does not have the Spirit of Christ, he does not belong to Christ. –* Romans 8:9

The Holy Spirit is called THE SPIRIT OF CHRIST. The Spirit of Christ in this passage does not mean a Christlike spirit. It means something far more than that, it means that which lies behind a Christlike spirit; it is a name of the Holy Spirit. Why is the Holy Spirit called THE SPIRIT OF CHRIST? For several reasons:

1) Because He is Christ's gift

The Holy Spirit is not merely the gift of the Father, but the gift of the Son as well.

> *And with that he breathed on them and said, "Receive the Holy Spirit." –* John 20:22

The Holy Spirit is the breath of Christ, as well as the breath of God the Father. It is Christ who breathes upon us and imparts to us the Holy Spirit. In John 14:15 and the following verses Jesus teaches us that it is in answer to His prayer that the Father gives to us the Holy Spirit.

> *Exalted to the right hand of God, he has received from the Father the promised Holy Spirit and <u>has poured out what you now see and hear</u>. –* Acts 2:33

Jesus, having been exalted to the right hand of God, in answer to His prayer, receives the Holy Spirit from the Father and pours forth upon the Church the Holy Spirit whom He has received from the Father. In Matthew 3:11 we read that it is Jesus who baptizes with the Holy Spirit. In John 7:37-39 Jesus bids all that are thirsty to COME TO ME and drink, and the context makes it clear that the water that He gives is the Holy Spirit, who becomes in those who receive Him a source of life and power flowing out to others. It is the glorified Christ who gives to the Church the Holy Spirit. In John 4:10 Jesus declares that He is the One who gives the living water, the Holy Spirit. In all these passages, Christ is set forth as the One who gives the Holy Spirit, so the Holy Spirit is called "the Spirit of Christ."

2) Because it is the work of the Holy Spirit to reveal Christ in us.

> *"He will bring glory to me by taking from what is mine and <u>making it known to you</u>." –* John 16:14

> *"When the Counselor comes, whom I will send to you from the Father, the Spirit of truth who goes out from the Father, <u>he will testify about me</u>." –* John 15:26

This is the work of the Holy Spirit to bear witness to Christ and reveal Jesus Christ to men. And as the revealer of Christ, He is called "the Spirit of Christ."

> 3) Because it is His work to form Christ as a living presence within us.

> *I pray that out of his glorious riches he may <u>strengthen you with power through his Spirit in your inner being</u>, so that Christ may dwell in your hearts through faith.* – Ephesians 3:16-17a

This is the work of the Holy Spirit – to cause Christ to dwell in our hearts, to form the living Christ within us. Just as the Holy Spirit literally and physically formed Jesus Christ in the womb of the Virgin Mary (Luke 1:35) so the Holy Spirit spiritually but really forms Jesus Christ within our hearts today. In John 14:16-18, Jesus told His disciples that when the Holy Spirit came that He Himself would come, that is, the result of the coming of the Holy Spirit to dwell in their hearts would be the coming of Christ Himself. It is the privilege of every believer in Christ to have the living Christ formed by the power of the Holy Spirit in his own heart and therefore the Holy Spirit who forms Christ within the heart is called the Spirit of Christ. How wonderful! How glorious is the significance of this name. Let us consider it until we understand it, as far as it is possible to understand it, and until we rejoice exceedingly in the glory of it.

7. *The Spirit of Jesus Christ.*

> *For I know that through your prayers and the help given by <u>the Spirit of Jesus Christ</u>, what has happened to me will turn out for my deliverance.* – Philippians 1:19

The Spirit is not merely the Spirit of the eternal Word but the Spirit of the Word incarnate. Not merely the Spirit of Christ, but the Spirit OF JESUS CHRIST. It is the Man Jesus exalted to the right hand of the Father who receives and sends the Spirit.

God has raised this Jesus to life, and we are all witnesses of the fact. Exalted to the right hand of God, he has received from the Father the promised Holy Spirit and has poured out what you now see and hear. – Acts 2:32-33

8. *The Spirit of Jesus.*

Paul and his companions traveled throughout the region of Phrygia and Galatia, having been kept by the Holy Spirit from preaching the word in the province of Asia. When they came to the border of Mysia, they tried to enter Bithynia, but the Spirit of Jesus would not allow them to. – Acts 16:6-7

By the using of this name, "THE SPIRIT OF JESUS" the thought of the relation of the Spirit to the MAN JESUS is still more clear than in the name preceding this, the Spirit of Jesus Christ.

9. *The Spirit of His Son.*

Because you are sons, God sent the Spirit of his Son into our hearts, the Spirit who calls out, "Abba, Father." – Galatians 4:6

We see from the context (vv. 4-5) that this name is given to the Holy Spirit in special connection with His testifying to the sonship of the believer. It is "THE SPIRIT OF HIS SON" who testifies to our sonship. The thought is that the Holy Spirit is a Spirit who produces a sense of sonship in us. If we receive the Holy Spirit, we no longer think of God as if we were serving under constraint and bondage but we are sons living in joyous liberty. We do not fear God, we trust Him and rejoice in Him. When we receive the Holy Spirit, we do not receive a Spirit of bondage again to fear but a Spirit of adoption where we call out, Abba, Father (Romans 8:15). This name of the Holy Spirit is one of the most suggestive of all. We would do well to consider it until we realize the full significance of it. We will look at this further when we come to our study the work of the Holy Spirit.

10. *The Holy Spirit.*

This name is of very frequent occurrence, and the name with which most of us are most familiar. One of the most familiar passages in which the name is used is Luke 11:13:

> *"If you then, though you are evil, know how to give good gifts to your children, how much more will your Father in heaven give the Holy Spirit to those who ask him!"* – Luke 11:13

This name emphasizes the essential moral character of the Spirit. He is HOLY in Himself. We are so familiar with the name that we neglect to consider its significance. Oh, if we only realized more deeply and constantly that He is the HOLY Spirit. We would do well if we, as the seraphim in Isaiah's vision, would bow in His presence and cry, "Holy, holy, holy." Yet how thoughtlessly we tend to talk about Him and pray for Him. We pray for Him to come into our churches and into our hearts but what would He find if He should come there? Would He not find much that would be painful and agonizing to Him? What would we think if a prostitute from the worst part of the city would go to the purest woman in the city and invite her to come and live with her with no intention of changing her evil ways? But if this same prostitute would go to the purest and most Christlike woman and ask her to live with her with the intention of putting away everything that was vile and evil and giving to this holy and Christlike woman the entire control of the place, she would go. And as sinful and selfish and imperfect as we may be, the infinitely Holy Spirit is ready to come and take His dwelling in our heart if we will surrender to Him the absolute control of our lives, and allow Him to bring everything in thought and desire and feeling and purpose and imagination and action into conformity with His will. The infinitely Holy Spirit is ready to come into our churches, however imperfect and worldly they may be now, if we are willing to put the absolute control of everything in His hands. But let us never forget that He is THE HOLY Spirit, and when we pray for Him let us pray for Him as with that in mind.

11. *The Holy Spirit of Promise.*

And you also were included in Christ when you heard the word of truth, the gospel of your salvation. Having believed, you were marked in him with a seal, <u>the promised Holy Spirit</u>. – Ephesians 1:13

We have here the same name as that given above with the added thought that this Holy Spirit is the great promise of the Father and of the Son. The Holy Spirit is God's great all-inclusive promise for the present age; the one thing for which Jesus told the disciples to wait for after His ascension before they began His work was the promise of the Father, that is the Holy Spirit (Acts 1:4-5). The great promise of the Father until the coming of Christ was the coming atoning Savior and King, but when Jesus came and died His atoning death upon the cross of Calvary and arose and ascended to the right hand of the Father, then the second great promise of the Father was the Holy Spirit to take the place of our absent Lord.

12. *The Spirit of Holiness.*

And who through <u>the Spirit of holiness</u> was declared with power to be the Son of God by his resurrection from the dead: Jesus Christ our Lord. – Romans 1:4

At the first glance it may seem as if there were no essential difference between the two names the Holy Spirit and the Spirit of holiness. But there is a marked difference. The name of the Holy Spirit, as already said, emphasizes the essential moral character of the Spirit as holy, but the name of THE SPIRIT OF HOLINESS brings out the thought that the Holy Spirit is not merely holy in Himself but He imparts holiness to others. The perfect holiness which He Himself possesses He imparts to those who receive Him (1 Peter 1:2).

13. *The Spirit of Truth.*

The Holy Spirit is called THE SPIRIT OF TRUTH in John 14:16-17:

"And I will ask the Father, and he will give you another Counselor to be with you forever-- the Spirit of truth. The world cannot accept him, because it neither sees him nor knows him. But you know him, for he lives with you and will be in you." – John 14:16-17

The Holy Spirit is called the Spirit of truth because it is the work of the Holy Spirit to communicate truth, to impart truth, to those who receive Him. This comes out in the passage given above, and, if possible, it comes out even more clearly in John 16:13:

But when he, the Spirit of truth, comes, he will guide you into all truth. He will not speak on his own; he will speak only what he hears, and he will tell you what is yet to come. – John 16:13

All truth is from the Holy Spirit. It is only as He teaches us that we come to know the truth.

14. *The Spirit of Wisdom and Understanding.*

The Holy Spirit is called *the Spirit of wisdom and understanding* in Isaiah 11:2:

The Spirit of the LORD will rest on him-- the Spirit of wisdom and of understanding, the Spirit of counsel and of power, the Spirit of knowledge and of the fear of the LORD. – Isaiah 11:2

The significance of the name is so plain as to need no explanation. It is evident both from the words used and from the context that it is the work of the Holy Spirit to impart wisdom and understanding to those who receive Him.

15. *The Spirit of Counsel and Power.*

We find this name used of the Holy Spirit in the passage given under the preceding heading. The meaning of this name too is obvious, the Holy Spirit is called "the Spirit of counsel and of power" because He gives us counsel in all our plans and strength to carry them out (Acts 8:29; 16:6, 7; 1:8). It is our privilege to have God's own counsel in all our plans and God's strength in all the work that we undertake for

Him. We receive them by receiving the Holy Spirit, the Spirit of counsel and might.

16. *The Spirit of Knowledge and of the Fear of the Lord.*

This name also is used in the passage given above (Isaiah 11:2). The significance of this name is also obvious. It is the work of the Holy Spirit to impart knowledge to us and to instill in us a reverence for Yahweh, that reverence that reveals itself above all in obedience to His commandments. The one who receives the Holy Spirit finds his delight in the fear of the LORD. (Isaiah 11:3). The three suggestive names just given refer especially to the gracious work of the Holy Spirit in the servant of the Lord, that is Jesus Christ.

17. *The Spirit of Life.*

The Holy Spirit is called THE SPIRIT OF LIFE in Romans 8:2:

Because through Christ Jesus the law of the Spirit of life set me free from the law of sin and death. – Romans 8:2

The Holy Spirit is called the Spirit of life because it is His work to impart life (John 6:63, Ezekiel 37:1-10). In the context in which the name is found in the passage given above, beginning back in the seventh chapter of Romans, seventh verse, Paul is drawing a contrast between the law of Moses outside a man, holy and just and good, it is true, but impotent, and the living Spirit of God in the heart, imparting spiritual and moral life to the believer and enabling him to meet the requirements of the law of God, so that what the law alone could not do, in that it was weak through the flesh, the Spirit of God imparting life to the believer and dwelling in the heart enables him to do, so that the righteousness of the law is fulfilled in those who walk not after the flesh but after the Spirit. (Romans 8:2-4.) The Holy Spirit is therefore called "the Spirit of life," because He imparts spiritual life and consequent victory over sin to those who receive Him.

18. *The Spirit of Grace.*

The Holy Spirit is called "the Spirit of grace" in Hebrews 10:29:

> *How much more severely do you think a man deserves to be punished who has trampled the Son of God under foot, who has treated as an unholy thing the blood of the covenant that sanctified him, and who has insulted the Spirit of grace? –* Hebrews 10:29

This name brings out the fact that it is the Holy Spirit's work to administer and apply the grace of God: He Himself is gracious, it is true, but the name means far more than that, it means that He makes ours experimentally the manifold grace of God. It is only by the work of the Spirit of grace in our hearts that we are enabled to appropriate to ourselves that infinite fullness of grace that God has, from the beginning, bestowed upon us in Jesus Christ. It is ours from the beginning, as far as belonging to us is concerned, but it is only ours experimentally as we claim it by the power of the Spirit of grace.

19. *The Spirit of Grace and of Supplication.*

The Holy Spirit is called "the Spirit of grace and of supplication" in Zechariah 12:10:

> *"And I will pour out on the house of David and the inhabitants of Jerusalem <u>a spirit of grace and supplication</u>. They will look on me, the one they have pierced, and they will mourn for him as one mourns for an only child, and grieve bitterly for him as one grieves for a firstborn son." –* Zechariah 12:10

The phrase, "a Spirit of grace and of supplication" in this passage is beyond a doubt a name of the Holy Spirit. The name "the Spirit of grace" we have already had under the preceding heading, but here there is a further thought of that operation of grace that leads us to pray intensely. The Holy Spirit is so called because it is He that teaches to pray because all true prayer is in the Spirit (Jude 20). We of ourselves do not know how to pray as we should, but it is the work of the Holy Spirit of intercession to make intercession for us with groanings which cannot be uttered and to lead us out in prayer according to the will of God (Romans 8:26-27). The secret of all true and effective praying is knowing the Holy Spirit as the "Spirit of grace and of supplication."

20. *The Spirit of Glory.*

If you are insulted because of the name of Christ, you are blessed, for the Spirit of glory and of God rests on you. – 1 Peter 4:14

This name does not merely teach that the Holy Spirit is infinitely glorious Himself, but it rather teaches that He imparts the glory of God to us, just as the Spirit of truth imparts truth to us, and as the Spirit of life imparts life to us, and as the Spirit of wisdom and understanding and of counsel and might and knowledge and of the fear of the LORD imparts to us wisdom and understanding and counsel and might and knowledge and the fear of the LORD, and as the Spirit of grace applies and administers to us the manifold grace of God, so the Spirit of glory is the administrator to us of God's glory. In the immediately preceding verse we read:

But rejoice that you participate in the sufferings of Christ, so that you may be overjoyed when his glory is revealed. – 1 Peter 4:13

It is in this connection that He is called the Spirit of glory. We find a similar connection between the sufferings which we endure and the glory which the Holy Spirit imparts to us in Romans 8:16-17:

The Spirit himself testifies with our spirit that we are God's children. Now if we are children, then we are heirs--heirs of God and co-heirs with Christ, if indeed we share in his sufferings in order that we may also share in his glory. – Romans 8:16-17

The Holy Spirit is the administrator of glory as well as of grace, or rather of the grace that culminates in glory.

21. *The Eternal Spirit.*

The Holy Spirit is called "the eternal Spirit" in Hebrews 9:14:

How much more, then, will the blood of Christ, who through the eternal Spirit offered himself unblemished to God, cleanse our consciences from acts that lead to death, so that we may serve the living God! – Hebrews 9:14

The eternity and the Deity and infinite majesty of the Holy Spirit are brought out by this name.

22. *The Counselor (or Comforter).*

The Holy Spirit is called "the Counselor" over and over again in the Scriptures. For example in John 14:26, we read:

"But the Counselor, the Holy Spirit, whom the Father will send in my name, will teach you all things and will remind you of everything I have said to you." – John 14:26

And in John 15:26:

"When the Counselor comes, whom I will send to you from the Father, the Spirit of truth who goes out from the Father, he will testify about me." – John 15:26

The word translated "Counselor" in these passages means that, but it means much more beside. It is a word difficult to adequately translate into any one word in English. The translators of the Revised Version found difficulty in deciding with what word to translate the Greek word, so they have suggested in the margin of the Revised Version "advocate" "helper" and a simple transference of the Greek word into English, "Paraclete."

The word translated "Counselor" means literally, "one called alongside," that is one called to stand constantly by one's side and who is ever ready to stand by us and take our part in everything in which his help is needed. It is a wonderfully tender and expressive name for the Holy One. Sometimes when we think of THE HOLY SPIRIT, He seems to be so far away, but when we think of the Parakleetos, or in plain English our "Stand-byer" or our "part-taker," how near He is.

Up to the time that Jesus made this promise to the disciples, He Himself had been their Parakleetos. When they were in any emergency or difficulty they turned to Him. On one occasion, for example, the disciples were in doubt as to how to pray and they turned to Jesus and said, "Lord, teach us to pray." And the Lord taught them the wonderful prayer that has come down through the ages (Luke 11:1-4). On another occasion, Peter was sinking in the waves of Galilee and he cried, "Lord, save me," and immediately Jesus stretched forth His hand and caught him and saved him (Matthew 14:30-31). In every extremity they turned to Him. And now that Jesus has gone to the Father, we have another Person, just as Divine as He is, just as wise as He, just as strong as He, just as loving as He, just as tender as He is, just as ready and just as able to help, who is always right by our side. Yes, better yet, who dwells in our heart, who will take hold and help if we only trust Him to do it.

If the truth of the Holy Spirit as set forth in the name "Parakleetos" gets into our hearts and abides there, it will remove all loneliness forever – how can we ever be lonely when this best of all Friends is with us at all times?

And if this thought of the Holy Spirit as the ever-present Paraclete gets into our hearts and abides there, it will banish all fear forever. How can we be afraid in the face of any peril, if this Divine One is by our side to counsel us and to take our part? There may be a mob around us, or a threatening storm, but it doesn't matter. He stands between us and both the mob and the storm.

As we think of the Holy Spirit as the Paraclete there is also a cure for a breaking heart. How many aching, breaking hearts there are in this world of ours, so full of death and separation from those we most dearly love. How many women are there, who a few years ago, or a few months or a few weeks ago, had no care, no worry, because by her side was a Christian husband who was so wise and strong that the wife was able to trust him for almost everything, and she walked through life satisfied with his love and companionship. But one awful day, he was taken from her. She was left alone and all the cares and responsibilities. How empty that heart has been ever since; how empty the whole world has been. She has just dragged through her life and her duties as best she could with an aching and almost breaking heart. But there is One, if she only knew it, wiser and more loving than the tenderest husband, One willing to bear all the care and responsibilities of life for her, One who is able, if, she will only let Him, to fill every nook and corner of her empty and aching heart; that One is the Paraclete.

But it is in our work for our Master that the thought of the Holy Spirit as the Paraclete comes with the greatest helpfulness. Many hesitate to speak to others about accepting Christ. They are afraid they won't say the right thing, or they are afraid that they will do more harm than good. You certainly will if YOU do it, but if you will just believe in the Paraclete and trust Him to say it and to say it in His way, you will never do harm but always good. It may seem at the time that you have accomplished nothing, but perhaps years after you will find out you have accomplished much and even if you do not find it out in this world, you will find it out in eternity.

CHAPTER 5: THE HOLY SPIRIT CONVICTING THE WORLD OF SIN, RIGHTEOUSNESS, AND JUDGMENT

Our salvation begins experimentally with our being brought to a profound sense that we need a Savior. The Holy Spirit is the One who brings us to this realization of our need. We read in John 16:8-11:

> *"When he comes, he will convict the world of guilt in regard to sin and righteousness and judgment: in regard to sin, because men do not believe in me; in regard to righteousness, because I am going to the Father, where you can see me no longer; and in regard to judgment, because the prince of this world now stands condemned."* – John 16:8-11

1. *The Holy Spirit convicts us of sin.*

That is, the Holy Spirit convinces us of our error in respect to sin to produce a deep sense of personal guilt. We have the first recorded fulfillment of this promise in Acts 2:36-37:

> *"Therefore let all Israel be assured of this: God has made this Jesus, whom you crucified, both Lord and Christ." When the people heard this, <u>they were cut to the heart</u> and said to Peter and the other apostles, "Brothers, <u>what shall we do</u>?"* – Acts 2:36-37

The Holy Spirit had come just as Jesus had promised that He would and when He came He convicted the world of sin – He "cut to the heart" with a sense of their awful guilt in the rejection of their Lord and their Christ. If the Apostle Peter had spoken the same words the day before Pentecost, no such results would have followed; but now Peter was filled with the Holy Spirit (v. 4) and the Holy Spirit took Peter and his words and through the instrumentality of Peter and his words convicted his hearers.

The Holy Spirit is the only One who can convince men of sin. The natural heart is "deceitful above all things and desperately wicked," and there is nothing in which the inbred deceitfulness of our hearts comes out more clearly than in our estimations of ourselves. We are all of us sharp-sighted enough to the faults of others but we are all blind by nature to our own faults. Our blindness to our own shortcomings is oftentimes little short of ludicrous. We have a strange power of exaggerating our imaginary virtues and losing sight of all our defects. The longer and more thoroughly a person studies human nature, the more clearly he will see how hopeless the task is of convincing other men of sin. We cannot do it, nor has God left it for us to do it. He has put this work into the hands of One who is abundantly able to do it, the Holy Spirit.

One of the worst mistakes that we can make in our efforts to bring people to Christ is to try to convince them of sin in any power of our own. Unfortunately, it is one of the commonest mistakes we make. Preachers will stand in the pulpit and argue and reason with men to make them see and realize that they are sinners. They make it as plain as day; it is a wonder that their hearers do not see it; but they don't. Personal workers sit down beside an inquirer and reason with him, and bring forward passages of Scripture in a most skillful way, the very passages that are calculated to produce the effect desired and yet there is no result. Why? Because we are trying to do the Holy Spirit's work, the work that He alone can do, convince men of sin. If we would only keep in mind our own utter inability to convince men of sin, and cast ourselves upon Him and trust Him to do the work, we would see results.

But while we cannot convict men of sin, there is One who can, the Holy Spirit. He can convince the most hardened and blinded man of sin. He can change men and women from utter carelessness and indifference to a place where they are overwhelmed with a sense of their need of a Savior.

Yet, while it is the Holy Spirit who convinces men of sin, He does it through us. This comes out very clearly in the context of the passage before us:

> *"But I tell you the truth: It is for your good that I am going away. Unless I go away, the Counselor will not come to you; but if I go, I will send him to you."* – John 16:7

Then He goes on to say:

"When he comes, <u>he will convict the world</u> of guilt in regard to sin and righteousness and judgment." – John 16:8

That is, our Lord Jesus sends the Holy Spirit unto us (unto believers), and when He has come to us who are believers, <u>through us</u> He convicts the world. On the Day of Pentecost, it was the Holy Spirit who convinced the 3,000 of sin, but the Holy Spirit came to the group of believers and through them convinced the outside world. As far as the Holy Scriptures definitely tell us, the Holy Spirit has no way of getting at the unsaved world except through the agency of those who are already saved. Every conversion recorded in the Acts of the Apostles was through the agency of men or women already saved.

Take, for example, the conversion of Saul of Tarsus. If there ever was a miraculous conversion, it was that. The glorified Jesus appeared visibly to Saul on his way to Damascus, but before Saul could come out clearly into the light as a saved man, human instrumentality must be brought in. Saul prostrate on the ground cried to the risen Christ asking what he must do, and the Lord told him to go into Damascus and there he would be told what he must do. And then Ananias was brought on the scene as the human instrumentality through whom the Holy Spirit should do His work (see Acts 9:17; 22:12ff).

Take the case of Cornelius. Here again was a most remarkable conversion through supernatural agency. "AN ANGEL" appeared to Cornelius, but the angel did not tell Cornelius what to do to be saved. The angel rather said to Cornelius:

"Send to Joppa <u>for Simon</u> who is called Peter. <u>He</u> will bring you a message through which <u>you and all your household will be saved</u>." – Acts 11:13b-14

So we may go right through the record of the conversions in the Acts of the Apostles and we will see they were all effected through human instrumentality. How solemn, how almost overwhelming, is the thought that the Holy Spirit has no way of getting at the unsaved with His saving power except through the instrumentality of us who are already Christians. If we realized that, wouldn't we be more careful to offer to the Holy Spirit a more free and unobstructed channel for His all-important work? The Holy Spirit needs human lips to speak through. He needs yours, and He needs lives so clean and so utterly surrendered to Him that He can work through them.

Notice specifically which sin it is that the Holy Spirit convinces men of—the sin of unbelief in Jesus Christ, *"in regard to sin, because men do not believe in me,"* says Jesus. Not the sin of stealing, not the sin of drunkenness, not the sin of adultery, not the sin of murder, but the sin of unbelief in Jesus Christ. The one thing that the eternal God demands of men is that they believe on Him whom He has sent (John 6:29). And the one sin that reveals men's rebellion against God and daring defiance of Him is the sin of not believing in Jesus Christ, and this is the one sin that the Holy Spirit puts to the front and emphasizes and of which He convicts men. This was the sin of which He convicted the 3,000 on the Day of Pentecost. Doubtless, there were many other sins in their lives, but the one point that the Holy Spirit brought to the forefront through the Apostle Peter was that the One whom they had rejected was their Lord and Christ, attested to by His resurrection from the dead (Acts 2:22-36). "And *"when the people heard this* (namely, that He whom they had rejected was Lord and Christ) *they were cut to the heart."* This is the sin of which the Holy Spirit convicts us today. In regard to the comparatively minor moralities of life, there is a wide difference among men, but the thief who rejects Christ and the honest man who rejects Christ are alike condemned at the great point of what they do with God's Son, and this is the point that the Holy Spirit presses home.

The sin of unbelief is the most difficult of all sins of which to convince men. The average unbeliever does not look upon unbelief as a sin. Many an unbeliever looks upon his unbelief as a mark of intellectual superiority. Not infrequently, he is all the more proud of it because it is the only mark of intellectual superiority that he possesses. He tosses his head and says, "I am an agnostic;" "I am a skeptic;" or, "I am an infidel," and assumes an air of superiority on that account. If he does not go so far as that, the unbeliever frequently looks upon his unbelief as, at the very worst, a misfortune. He looks for pity rather than for blame. He says, "Oh, I wish I could believe. I am so sorry I cannot believe," and then appeals to us for pity because he cannot believe, but when the Holy Spirit touches a man's heart, he no longer looks upon unbelief as a mark of intellectual superiority; he does not look upon it as a mere misfortune; he sees it as the most daring, decisive and damning of all sins and is overwhelmed with a sense of his awful guilt in that he had not believed on the name of the only begotten Son of God.

2. *The Holy Spirit convicts in respect to righteousness.*

He convicts the world in respect to righteousness because Jesus Christ has gone to the Father, that is He convicts (convinces with a convincing that is self-condemning) the world of Christ's righteousness attested to by His going to the Father. The coming of the Spirit is in itself a proof that Christ has gone to the Father (see Acts 2:33) and the Holy Spirit opens our eyes to see that Jesus Christ, whom the world condemned as an evil-doer, was indeed the righteous One. The Father sets the stamp of His approval upon His character and claims by raising Him from the dead and exalting Him to His own right hand and giving to Him a name that is above every name. The world at large today claims to believe in the righteousness of Christ but it does not really believe in the righteousness of Christ: it has no adequate conception of the righteousness of Christ. The righteousness which the world attributes to Christ is not the righteousness which God attributes to Him, but a poor human righteousness, perhaps a little better than our own. The world loves to put the names of other men that it considers good alongside the name of Jesus Christ. But when the Spirit of God comes to a man, He convinces him of the righteousness of Christ; He opens his eyes to see Jesus Christ standing absolutely alone, not only far above all men but:

> *Far above all rule and authority, power and dominion, and every title that can be given, not only in the present age but also in the one to come.* – Ephesians 1:21

3. *The Holy Spirit convicts the world of judgment.*

The ground upon which the Holy Spirit convinces men of judgment is upon the ground of the fact that:

"The prince of this world now stands condemned." – John 16:11a

When Jesus Christ was nailed to the cross, it seemed as if He were judged there, but in reality it was the Prince of this world who was judged at the cross, and, by raising Jesus Christ from the dead, the Father made it plain to all coming ages that the cross was not the judgment of Christ, but the judgment of the Prince of darkness. The Holy Spirit opens our eyes to see this fact and so convinces us of judgment. There is a great need today that the world be convinced of judgment. Judgment is a doctrine that has fallen into the background, that has indeed almost sunken out of sight. It is not popular today to speak about judgment, or retribution, or hell. A person who emphasizes judgment and future retribution is not thought to be quite up to date; he is considered "behind the times" or even "archaic," but when the Holy Spirit opens the eyes of men, they believe in judgment.

CHAPTER 6: THE HOLY SPIRIT BEARING WITNESS TO JESUS CHRIST

When our Lord was talking to His disciples on the night before His crucifixion of the Counselor who would come to take His place, He said:

> *"When the Counselor comes, whom I will send to you from the Father, the Spirit of truth who goes out from the Father, he will testify about me. And you also must testify, for you have been with me from the beginning."* – John 15:26-27

Later, when the Apostle Peter and the other disciples were strictly commanded by the Jewish Council not to teach in the name of Jesus they said:

> *We are witnesses of these things, and so is the Holy Spirit, whom God has given to those who obey him."* – Acts 5:32

1. *The Holy Spirit bears witness to our hearts.*

It is clear from these words of Jesus Christ and the Apostles that it is the work of the Holy Spirit to bear witness concerning Jesus Christ. We find the Holy Spirit's testimony to Jesus Christ in the Scriptures, but beside this the Holy Spirit bears witness directly to the individual heart concerning Jesus Christ. He takes His own Scriptures and interprets them to us and makes them clear to us. All truth is from the Spirit, for He is "the Spirit of truth," but it is especially His work to bear witness to Him who is the truth, that is Jesus Christ (John 14:6).

It is only through the testimony of the Holy Spirit directly to our hearts that we ever come to a true, living knowledge of Jesus Christ (see 1 Corinthians 12:3). No amount of mere reading the written Word (in the Bible) and no amount of listening to man's testimony will ever bring us to a living knowledge of Christ. It is only when the Holy Spirit Himself takes the written Word, or takes the testimony of our fellow man, and interprets it directly to our hearts that we really come to see and know Jesus as He is. On the day of Pentecost, Peter gave all his hearers the testimony of the Scriptures regarding Christ and also gave them his own testimony; he told them what he and the other Apostles knew by personal observation regarding His resurrection, but unless the Holy Spirit Himself had taken the Scriptures which Peter had brought together and taken the testimony of Peter and the other disciples, the 3,000 would not on that day have seen Jesus as He really was and received Him and been baptized in His name. The Holy Spirit added His testimony to that of Peter and that of the written Word. D.L. Moody used to say in his terse and graphic way that when Peter said, "Therefore let all the house of Israel know assuredly that God hath made that same Jesus, whom ye have crucified, both Lord and Christ (Acts 2:36), the Holy Spirit said, 'Amen' and the people saw and believed." And it is certain that unless the Holy Spirit had come that day and through Peter and the other Apostles bearing His direct testimony to the hearts of their hearers, there would have been no saving vision of Jesus on the part of the people.

2. *The Holy Spirit bears witness through us.*

If you desire for people to get a true view of Jesus Christ, such a view of Him that they may believe and be saved, it is not enough that you give them the Scriptures concerning Him; it is not enough that you give them your own testimony, you must seek for them the testimony of the Holy Spirit and put yourself into such a relationship with God that the Holy Spirit may bear His testimony through you. Neither your testimony, nor even that of the written Word alone will effect this, though it is your testimony, or that of the Word that the Holy Spirit uses. But unless your testimony and that of the Word is taken up by the Holy Spirit and He Himself testifies, they will not believe.

This explains something which every experienced evangelist must have noticed. We sit down beside an inquirer and open our Bibles and give him those Scriptures which clearly reveal Jesus as his atoning Savior on the cross, a Savior from the guilt of sin, and as his risen Savior, a Savior from the power of sin. It is just the truth the man needs to see and believe in order to be saved, but he does not see it. We go over these Scriptures which to us are as plain as day again and again, and the inquirer sits there in blank darkness; he sees nothing, he grasps nothing. Sometimes we almost wonder if the inquirer is stupid because he cannot see it. But no, he is not stupid, except with that spiritual blindness that possesses every mind unenlightened by the Holy Spirit (1 Corinthians 2:14). We go over it again and still he does not see it. We go over it again and his face lightens up and he exclaims, "I see it. I see it," and he sees Jesus and believes and is saved and knows he is saved there on the spot. What has happened? Simply this, the Holy Spirit has given His testimony and what was dark as midnight before is as clear as day now.

This also explains why it is that one who has been long in darkness concerning Jesus Christ so quickly comes to see the truth when he surrenders his will to God and seeks light from Him. When he surrenders his will to God, he has put himself into that attitude towards God where the Holy Spirit can do His work (Acts 5:32).

> *"If anyone chooses to do God's will, he will find out whether my teaching comes from God or whether I speak on my own."*
> – John 7:17

3. *The Holy Spirit bears witness through the Word of God.*

When a man wills to do the will of God, then the conditions are provided on which the Holy Spirit works and He illuminates the mind to see the truth about Jesus and to see that His teaching is the very Word of God.

> *But these are written that you may believe that Jesus is the Christ, the Son of God, and that by believing you may have life in his name.* – John 20:31

John wrote his Gospel for this purpose, that men might see Jesus as the Christ, the Son of God, through what he records, and that they might believe that He is the Christ, the Son of God, and that thus believing they might have life through His name. The best book in the world to put into the hands of one who desires to know about Jesus and to be saved is the Gospel of John. And yet many a man has read the Gospel of John over and over and over again and not seen and believed that Jesus is the Christ, the Son of God. But let the same man surrender his will absolutely to God and ask God for light as he reads the Gospel and promise God that he will take his stand on everything in the Gospel that He shows him to be true and before the man has finished the Gospel he will see clearly that Jesus is the Christ, the Son of God, and will believe and have eternal life. Why? Because he has put himself into the place where the Holy Spirit can take the things written in the Gospel and interpret them and bear His testimony.

If you wish for people to see the truth about Christ, do not depend upon your own powers of expression and persuasion, but cast yourself upon the Holy Spirit and seek for them His testimony and see to it that they put themselves in the place where the Holy Spirit can testify. This is the cure for both skepticism and ignorance concerning Christ. If you yourself are not clear concerning the truth about Jesus Christ, seek for yourself the testimony of the Holy Spirit regarding Christ. Read the Scriptures, read especially the Gospel of John but do not depend upon the mere reading of the Word, but before you read it, put yourself in such an attitude towards God by the absolute surrender of your will to Him that the Holy Spirit may bear His testimony in your heart concerning Jesus Christ. What we all most need is a clear and full vision of Jesus Christ and this comes through the testimony of the Holy Spirit. It is our part to hold up Jesus Christ, and then look to the Holy Spirit to illumine His face or to take the truth about Him and make it clear to the hearts of our hearers and He will do it and men will see and believe. Of course, we need to be so walking towards God that the Holy Spirit may take us as the instruments through whom He will bear His testimony.

CHAPTER 7: THE REGENERATING WORK OF THE HOLY SPIRIT

He saved us, not because of righteous things we had done, but because of his mercy. He saved us through the washing of rebirth and <u>renewal by the Holy Spirit</u>. – Titus 3:5

In these words we are taught that THE HOLY SPIRIT RENEWS MEN, OR MAKES MEN NEW, and that through this renewing of the Holy Spirit, we are saved. Jesus taught the same in John 3:3-5:

In reply Jesus declared, "I tell you the truth, no one can see the kingdom of God unless he is born again." "How can a man be born when he is old?" Nicodemus asked. "Surely he cannot enter a second time into his mother's womb to be born!" Jesus answered, "I tell you the truth, no one can enter the kingdom of God unless he is born of water <u>and the Spirit</u>." – John 3:3-5

What is regeneration?

1. Regeneration is the impartation of spiritual life to those who are spiritually dead through their trespasses and sins (Eph. 2:1).

It is the Holy Spirit who imparts this life. It is true that the written Word is the instrument which the Holy Spirit uses in regeneration.

For you have been born again, not of perishable seed, but of imperishable, <u>through the living and enduring word of God</u>. – 1 Peter 1:23

He chose to give us birth through <u>the word of truth</u>, that we might be a kind of firstfruits of all he created. – James 1:18

These passages make it plain that the Word is the instrument used in regeneration, but it is only as the Holy Spirit uses the instrument that the new birth results.

"The Spirit gives life; the flesh counts for nothing. The words I have spoken to you are spirit and they are life." – John 6:63

He has made us competent as ministers of a new covenant--not of the letter but of the Spirit; for the letter kills, but the Spirit gives life. – 2 Corinthians 3:6

This is sometimes interpreted to mean that the literal interpretation of Scripture, the interpretation that takes it in its strict grammatical sense and makes it mean what it says, kills; but that some spiritual interpretation, an interpretation that "gives the spirit of the passage," by making it mean something it does not say, gives life; and those who insist upon Scripture meaning exactly what it says are called "fundamentalists" or "literalists." This is a favorite perversion of Scripture with those who do not like to take the Bible as meaning just what it says and who find themselves driven into a corner and are looking about for some convenient way of escape. If one will read the words in their context, he will see that this thought was utterly foreign to the mind of Paul. Indeed, one who will carefully study the epistles of Paul will find that he himself was a literalist of the literalists. If literalism is deadly, then the teachings of Paul are among the most deadly ever written. Paul will build an argument upon the turn of a word, upon a number or a tense. What does the passage mean? The way to find out what any passage means is to study in their context the words used. Paul is drawing a contrast between the Word of God outside of us, written with ink upon parchment or graven on tables of stone, and the Word of God written within us in tables that are hearts of flesh with the Spirit of the living God (v. 3) and he tells us that if we merely have the Word of God outside us in a Book or on parchment or on tables of stone, that it will kill us, that it will only bring condemnation and death, but that if we have the Word of God made a living thing in our hearts, written upon our hearts by the Spirit of the living God, that it will bring us life. No number of Bibles upon our tables or in our libraries will save us, but the truth of the Bible written by the Spirit of the living God in our hearts will save us.

To put the matter of regeneration in another way;

2. Regeneration is the impartation of a new nature – God's own nature – to the one who is born again.

Through these he has given us his very great and precious promises, so that through them you may participate in the divine nature and escape the corruption in the world caused by evil desires. – 2 Peter 1:4

Every human being is born into this world with a perverted nature; his whole intellectual, affectional and volitional nature perverted by sin. No matter how excellent our human ancestry, we come into this world with a mind that is blind to the truth of God.

The man without the Spirit does not accept the things that come from the Spirit of God, for they are foolishness to him, and he cannot understand them, because they are spiritually discerned. – 1 Corinthians 2:14

We come into this world with affections that are alienated from God, loving the things that we ought to hate and hating the things that we ought to love.

The acts of the sinful nature are obvious: sexual immorality, impurity and debauchery; idolatry and witchcraft; hatred, discord, jealousy, fits of rage, selfish ambition, dissensions, factions and envy; drunkenness, orgies, and the like. I warn you, as I did before, that those who live like this will not inherit the kingdom of God. – Galatians 5:19-21

We come into this world with a will that is perverted, set upon pleasing itself, rather than pleasing God.

The sinful mind is hostile to God. It does not submit to God's law, nor can it do so. – Romans 8:7

The good news is that in the new birth a new intellectual, affectional and volitional nature is imparted to us. We receive the mind that sees as God sees, and thinks God's thoughts after Him.

We have not received the spirit of the world but the Spirit who is from God, that we may understand what God has freely given us. This is what we speak, not in words taught us by human wisdom but in words taught by the Spirit, expressing spiritual truths in spiritual words. – 1 Corinthians 2:12-13

We now have affections in harmony with the affections of God.

But the fruit of the Spirit is love, joy, peace, patience, kindness, goodness, faithfulness, gentleness and self-control. Against such things there is no law. Those who belong to Christ Jesus have crucified the sinful nature with its passions and desires. – Galatians 5:22-24

We now have a will that is in harmony with the will of God, and that delights in doing the things that please Him. Like Jesus we say:

"My food is to do the will of him who sent me and to finish his work." – John 4:34

(see John 6:38; Galatians 1:10) It is the Holy Spirit who creates in us this new nature, or imparts this new nature to us. No amount of preaching, no matter how orthodox it may be, no amount of mere study of the Word will regenerate unless the Holy Spirit works. It is He and He alone who makes a man a new creature.

The new birth is compared in the Bible to growth from a seed. The human heart is the soil, the Word of God is the seed (see Luke 8:11; 1 Peter 1:23; James 1:18), every preacher or teacher of the Word is a sower, but the Spirit of God is the One who breathes life into the seed that is sown and the Divine nature springs up as the result. There is abundant soil everywhere in which to sow the seed, in the human hearts that are around us on every hand. There is abundant seed to be sown, any of us can find it in the granary of God's Word; and there are today many sowers: but there may be soil and seed and sowers, but unless as we sow the seed, the Spirit of God brings it to life and the heart of the hearer closes around it by faith, there will be no harvest. Every sower needs to see to it that he realizes his dependence upon the Holy Spirit to nurture the seed he sows and he needs to see to it that he is in such relationship with God that the Holy Spirit may work through him.

3. *The Holy Spirit regenerates us*.

He has power to raise the dead. He has power to impart life to those who are morally both dead and putrefying. He has power to impart an entirely new nature to those whose nature now is so corrupt that to men they appear to be beyond hope. Conversion is merely an outward thing, the turning around. Regeneration goes down to the deepest depths of the inmost soul, transforming thoughts, affections, will, the whole inward man. The Christianity God has revealed in His Word and the Christianity that God confirms in experience teaches sudden regeneration by the mighty power of the Holy Spirit. If I did not believe in regeneration by the power of the Holy Spirit, I would quit preaching and teaching. What would be the use in facing audiences in which there were multitudes of men and women hardened and seared, caring for nothing but the things of the world and the flesh, with no high and holy aspirations, with no outlook beyond money and fame and power and pleasure, if it were not for the regenerating power of the Holy Spirit? But with the regenerating power of the Holy Spirit, there is every use; for the preacher or teacher can never tell where the Spirit of God is going to strike and do His mighty work. There sits before you a man who is a gambler, or a drunk, or an adulterer. There does not seem to be much use in teaching him, but you can never tell that that very night, the Spirit of God will touch that man's heart and transform him into one of the holiest and most useful of men. It has often occurred in the past and will doubtless often occur in the future. There sits before you a woman, who is living very far away from God. She seems to have no thought above her everyday life and pleasure. Why preach to her? Without the regenerating power of the Holy Spirit, it would be foolishness and a waste of time; but you can never tell, perhaps this very night the Spirit of God will shine in that darkened heart and open the eyes of that woman to see the beauty of Jesus Christ and she may receive Him and then and there the life of God be imparted by the power of the Holy Spirit to her soul.

The doctrine of the regenerating power of the Holy Spirit is a glorious doctrine. It sweeps away false hopes. It comes to the one who is trusting in education and culture and says, "Education and culture are not enough. You must be born again." It comes to the one who is trusting in mere external morality, and says, "External morality is not enough, you must be born again." It comes to the one who is trusting in the externalities of religion, in going to church, reading the Bible, saying prayers, being confirmed, being baptized, partaking of the Lord's supper, and says, "The mere externalities of religion are not enough, you must be born again." It comes to the one who is trusting in turning over a new leaf, in outward reform, in quitting his meanness; it says, "Outward reform, quitting your meanness is not enough. You must be born again." But in place of the vague and shallow hopes that it sweeps away, it brings in a new hope, a good hope, a blessed hope, a glorious hope. It says, "You may be born again." It comes to the one who has no desire higher than the desire for things animal or selfish or worldly and says, "You may become a partaker of the Divine nature, and love the things that God loves and hate the things that God hates. You may become like Jesus Christ. You may be born again."

CHAPTER 8: THE INDWELLING SPIRIT FULLY AND FOREVER SATISFYING

1. *The Holy Spirit takes up His abode in the one who is born of the Spirit.*

> *Don't you know that you yourselves are God's temple and that God's Spirit lives in you? If anyone destroys God's temple, God will destroy him; for God's temple is sacred, and you are that temple. – 1 Corinthians 3:16-17*

This passage refers, not so much to the individual believer, as to the whole body of believers, the Church. The Church as a body is indwelt by the Spirit of God. But in 1 Corinthians 6:19 we read:

> *Do you not know that your body is a temple of the Holy Spirit, who is in you, whom you have received from God? You are not your own. – 1 Corinthians 6:19*

It is evident in this passage that Paul is not speaking of the body of believers, of the Church as a whole, but of the individual believer. In a similar way, the Lord Jesus said to His disciples on the night before His crucifixion:

> *"And I will ask the Father, and he will give you another Counselor to be with you forever-- the Spirit of truth. The world cannot accept him, because it neither sees him nor knows him. But you know him, for he lives with you and will be in you." – John 14:16-17*

The Holy Spirit dwells in everyone who is born again.

> *You, however, are controlled not by the sinful nature but by the Spirit, if the Spirit of God lives in you. And if anyone does not have the Spirit of Christ, he does not belong to Christ. – Romans 8:9*

One may be a very imperfect believer but if he really is a believer in Jesus Christ, if he has really been born again, the Spirit of God dwells in him. It is very evident from the First Epistle to the Corinthians that the believers in Corinth were very imperfect believers; they were full of imperfection and there was gross sin among them. But nevertheless Paul tells them that they are temples of the Holy Spirit, even when dealing with them concerning gross immoralities. (See 1 Cor. 6:15-19.) *THE HOLY SPIRIT DWELLS IN EVERY CHILD OF GOD*. In some, however, He dwells way back of consciousness in the hidden sanctuary of their spirit. He is not allowed to take possession as He desires of the whole man, spirit, soul and body. Some therefore are not distinctly conscious of His indwelling, but He is there none the less. What a solemn, and yet what a glorious thought, that in me dwells this majestic Person, the Holy Spirit. If we are children of God, we are not so much to pray that the Spirit may come and dwell in us, for He does that already, we are rather to recognize His presence, His gracious and glorious indwelling, and give Him complete control of the house He already inhabits, and strive to live so as not to grieve this holy One, this Divine Guest. What a thought it gives of the hallowedness and sacredness of the body, to think of the Holy Spirit dwelling within us. How considerately we ought to treat these bodies and how sensitively we ought to shun everything that will defile them. How carefully we ought to walk in all things so as not to grieve Him who dwells within us.

2. This indwelling Spirit is a source of full and everlasting satisfaction and life.

Jesus was talking to the woman of Samaria by the well at Sychar. She had asked Him:

> *"Are you greater than our father Jacob, who gave us the well and drank from it himself, as did also his sons and his flocks and herds?" Jesus answered, "Everyone who drinks this water will be thirsty again." "But whoever drinks the water I give him will never thirst. Indeed, the water I give him will become in him a spring of water welling up to eternal life."* – John 4:12-14

How true that is of every earthly fountain. No matter how deeply we drink we shall thirst again. No earthly spring of satisfaction ever fully satisfies. We may drink of the fountain of wealth as deeply as we can, it will not satisfy long. We will be thirsty again. We may drink of the fountain of fame as deeply as any man ever drank, but the satisfaction is only for an hour. We may drink of the fountain of worldly pleasure, of human science and philosophy and of earthly learning, we may even drink of the fountain of human love, but none will satisfy long; we will thirst again.

But Jesus said, *"whoever drinks the water I give him will never thirst. Indeed, the water I give him will become in him a spring of water welling up to eternal life."* The water that Jesus Christ gives is the Holy Spirit. This John tells us in the most explicit language in John 7:37-39:

> *On the last and greatest day of the Feast, Jesus stood and said in a loud voice, "If anyone is thirsty, let him come to me and drink. Whoever believes in me, as the Scripture has said, streams of living water will flow from within him." By this he meant the Spirit, whom those who believed in him were later to receive. Up to that time the Spirit had not been given, since Jesus had not yet been glorified.* – John 7:37-39

The Holy Spirit fully and forever satisfies the one who receives Him. He becomes within him a well of water springing up, ever springing up, into everlasting life. It is a great thing to have a well that you can carry with you; to have a well that is within you; to have your source of satisfaction, not in the things outside yourself, but in a well within and that is always within, and that is always springing up in freshness and power; to have our well of satisfaction and joy within us. We are then independent of our environment.

It doesn't matter whether we have health or sickness, prosperity or adversity, our source of joy is within and is ever springing up. It matters comparatively little even whether we have our friends with us or are separated from them, separated even by what men call death, this fountain within is always gushing up and our souls are satisfied. Sometimes this fountain within gushes up with greatest power and fullness in the days of deepest bereavement. At such a time all earthly satisfactions fail. What satisfaction is there in money, or worldly pleasure, in fame or power or human learning, when some loved one is taken from us? But in the hours when those that we loved dearest upon earth are taken from us, then it is that the spring of joy of the indwelling Spirit of God bursts forth with fullest flow, sorrow and sighing flee away and our own spirits are filled with peace and ecstasy. We have beauty for ashes, the oil of joy for mourning, the garment of praise for the spirit of heaviness (Isaiah 61:3).

3. *The one who has the Spirit of God dwelling within is set free from the power of sin.*

Therefore, there is now no condemnation for those who are in Christ Jesus, because through Christ Jesus the law of the Spirit of life set me free from the law of sin and death. – Romans 8:1-2

We learn what the law of sin and death is from the preceding chapter (Romans 7:9-24). Paul tells us that there was a time in his life when he was alive apart from the law.

Once I was alive apart from law; but when the commandment came, sin sprang to life and I died. – Romans 7:9

But the time came when Paul was brought face to face with the law of God; he saw that this law was holy and the commandment holy and just and good. And he made up his mind to keep this holy and just and good law of God. But he soon discovered that beside this law of God outside him, which was holy and just and good, that there was another law inside him directly contrary to this law of God outside him. While the law of God outside him said, "This good thing" and "this good thing" and "this good thing" and "this good thing you will do," the law within him said, "You cannot do this good thing;" and a fierce combat ensued between this holy and just and good law without him which Paul himself approved after the inward man, and this other law in his members which warred against the law of his mind and kept constantly saying, "You cannot do this good thing." But this law in his members (the law that the good that he would do, he did not, but the evil that he would not he constantly did, v. 19) gained the victory. Paul's attempt to keep the law of God resulted in total failure. He found himself sinking deeper and deeper into the mire of sin, constrained and dragged down by this law of sin in his members, until at last he cried out:

What a wretched man I am! Who will rescue me from this body of death? – Romans 7:24

Then Paul made another discovery. He found that in addition to the two laws that he had already found, the law of God without him, holy and just and good, and the law of sin and death within him, there was a third law, "the law of the Spirit of life" in Christ Jesus, and this third law read this way, "The righteousness which you cannot achieve in your own strength by the power of your own will approving the law of God, the righteousness which the law of God without you, holy and just and good though it is, cannot accomplish in you, in that it is weak through your flesh, the Spirit of life in Christ Jesus can produce in you so that the righteousness that the law requires may be fulfilled in you, if you will not walk after the flesh but after the Spirit." In other words when we come to the end of ourselves, when we fully realize our own inability to keep the law of God and in utter helplessness look up to the Holy Spirit in Christ Jesus to do for us what we cannot do for ourselves, and surrender our every thought and every purpose and every desire and every affection to His absolute control and walk after the Spirit, the Spirit takes control and sets us free from the power of sin that dwells in us and brings our whole lives into conformity to the will of God. *IT IS THE PRIVILEGE OF THE CHILD OF GOD IN THE POWER OF THE HOLY SPIRIT TO HAVE VICTORY OVER SIN EVERY DAY AND EVERY HOUR AND EVERY MOMENT.*

There are many professed Christians today living in the experience that Paul described in Romans 7:9-24. Each day is a day of defeat and if at the close of the day, they review their lives they must cry, "Oh, wretched man that I am, who shall deliver me out of the body of this death?" There are some who even go so far as to reason that this is the normal Christian life, but Paul tells us distinctly that this was "when the commandment came" (v. 9), not when the Spirit came; that it is the experience under law and not in the Spirit. The pronoun "I" occurs twenty-seven times in these fifteen verses and the Holy Spirit is not found once, whereas in the eighth chapter of Romans the pronoun "I" is found only twice in the whole chapter and the Holy Spirit appears constantly. Again Paul tells us in the fourteenth verse that this was his experience as "unspiritual, sold as a slave to sin." Certainly, that does not describe the normal Christian experience.

On the other hand in Romans 8:9 we are told how not to be in the flesh but in the Spirit. In the eighth chapter of Romans we have a picture of the true Christian life, the life that is possible to each one of us and that God expects from each one of us. Here we have a life where not merely the commandment comes but the Spirit comes, and works obedience to the commandment and brings us complete victory over the law of sin and death. Here we have life, not in the flesh, but in the Spirit, where we not only see the beauty of the law (Romans 7:22) but where the Spirit imparts power to keep it (Romans 8:4). We still have the flesh but we are not in the flesh and we do not live after the flesh.

> *For if you live according to the sinful nature, you will die; but if by the Spirit <u>you put to death the misdeeds of the body</u>, you will live.* – Romans 8:13

The desires of the body are still there, desires which if made the rule of our life, would lead us into sin, but we day by day by the power of the Spirit put to death the deeds to which the desires of the body would lead us. We walk by the Spirit and therefore do not fulfill the lusts of the flesh (Galatians 5:16). We have crucified the flesh with its passions and desires (Galatians 5:24). It would be GOING TOO FAR TO SAY WE HAD STILL A CARNAL NATURE, for a carnal nature is a nature governed by the flesh; BUT WE HAVE THE FLESH, but in the Spirit's power, it is our privilege to get daily, hourly, constant victory over the flesh and over sin. But this victory is not in ourselves, nor in any strength of our own. Left to ourselves, deserted of the Spirit of God, we would be as helpless as ever. It is still true that in us, that is in our flesh, dwells no good thing (Romans 7:18). It is all in the power of the indwelling Spirit, but the Spirit's power may be in such fullness that one is not even conscious of the presence of the flesh. It seems as if it were dead and gone forever, but it is only kept in place of death by the Holy Spirit's power. If for one moment we were to get our eyes off from Jesus Christ, if we were to neglect the daily study of the Word and prayer, down we would go. We must live in the Spirit and walk in the Spirit if we would have continuous victory (Galatians 5:16, 25).

The life of the Spirit within us must be maintained by the study of the Word and prayer. One of the saddest things ever witnessed is the way in which some people who have entered by the Spirit's power into a life of victory become self-confident and begin to believe that the victory is in themselves, and that they can safely neglect the study of the Word and prayer. The depths to which they sometimes fall is appalling. Each of us needs to lay to heart the inspired words of the Apostle:

So, if you think you are standing firm, be careful that you don't fall! – 1 Corinthians 10:12

In John 8:32 we read:

"Then you will know the truth, and the truth will set you free." – John 8:32

In this verse it is the truth, or the Word of God, that sets us free from the power of sin and gives us victory.

I have hidden your word in my heart that I might not sin against you. – Psalms 119:11

Here again it is the indwelling Word that keeps us free from sin. In this matter as in everything else what in one place is attributed to the Holy Spirit is elsewhere attributed to the Word. The explanation, of course, is that the Holy Spirit works through the Word, and it is futile to talk of the Holy Spirit dwelling in us if we neglect the Word. If we are not feeding on the Word, we are not walking after the Spirit and we shall not have victory over the flesh and over sin.

CHAPTER 9: THE HOLY SPIRIT FORMING CHRIST WITHIN US

It is a wonderful and deeply significant prayer that Paul offers for the believers in Ephesus and for all believers who read the Epistle:

> *I pray that out of his glorious riches he may strengthen you with power through his Spirit in your inner being, so that Christ may dwell in your hearts through faith. And I pray that you, being rooted and established in love, may have power, together with all the saints, to grasp how wide and long and high and deep is the love of Christ, and to know this love that surpasses knowledge--that you may be filled to the measure of all the fullness of God.* – Ephesians 3:16-19

We have here an advance in the thought over what we have just been studying in the preceding chapter. It is the carrying out of the former work to its completion. Here the power of the Spirit manifests itself, not merely in giving us victory over sin but in four things:

1. *In Christ dwelling in our hearts.*

The word translated "dwell" in this passage is a very strong word. It means literally, "to dwell down," "to settle," "to dwell deep." It is the work of the Holy Spirit to form the living Christ within us, dwelling deep down in the deepest depths of our being. We have already seen that this was a part of the significance of the name sometimes used of the Holy Spirit, "the Spirit of Christ." In Christ on the cross of Calvary, made an atoning sacrifice for sin, bearing the curse of the broken law in our place, we have CHRIST FOR US. But by the power of the Holy Spirit bestowed upon us by the risen Christ we have CHRIST IN US. Herein lies the secret of a Christlike life. We hear a great deal in these days about doing as Jesus would do. Certainly, as Christians, we ought to live like Christ.

> *Whoever claims to live in him must walk as Jesus did.* – 1 John 2:6

But any attempt on our part to imitate Christ in our own strength will only result in utter disappointment and despair. There is nothing more futile that we can possibly attempt than to imitate Christ in the power of our own will. If we believe that we can succeed it will be simply because we have a very incomplete knowledge of Christ. The more we study Him, and the more perfectly we understand His conduct, the more clearly we will see how far short we have come from imitating Him. But God does not demand of us the impossible, He does not demand of us that we imitate Christ in our own strength. He offers to us something infinitely better, He offers to form Christ in us by the power of His Holy Spirit. And when Christ is formed in us by the Holy Spirit's power, all we have to do is to let this indwelling Christ live out His own life in us, and then we shall be like Christ without struggle and effort of our own. In and of ourselves we are full of weakness and failure, but the Holy Spirit is able to form within us the Holy One of God, the indwelling Christ, and He will live out His life through us in all the humblest relations of life as well as in those relations of life that are considered greater. He will live out His life through the mother in the home, through the laborer in the factory, through the business man in his office—everywhere.

2. *In our being rooted and established in love* (v. 17)

Paul multiplies figures here. The first figure is taken from the tree shooting its roots down deep into the earth and taking fast hold upon it. The second figure is taken from a great building with its foundations laid deep in the earth on the rock. Paul therefore tells us that by the strengthening of the Spirit in the inward man we send the roots of our life down deep into the soil of love and also that the foundations of the superstructure of our character are built upon the rock of love. Love is the sum of holiness, the fulfilling of the law (Romans 8:10); love is what we all most need in our relations to God, to Jesus Christ and to one another; and it is the work of the Holy Spirit to root and establish (or "ground") our lives in love. There is the most intimate relation between Christ being formed within us, or made to dwell in us, and our being rooted and grounded in love, for Jesus Christ Himself is the absolutely perfect embodiment of divine love.

3. *In our being given power to grasp with all the saints what is the width and length and height and depth of Christ's love, as well as to know the love of Christ which surpasses knowledge.*

It is not enough that we love, we must know the love of Christ, but that love surpasses knowledge. It is so broad, so long, so high, so deep, that no one can comprehend it. But we can "apprehend" it, we can lay hold upon it; we can make it our own; we can hold it before us as the object of our meditation, our wonder, and our joy. But it is only in the power of the Holy Spirit that we can do this. The mind cannot grasp it at all, in its own native strength. A man untaught and unstrengthened by the Spirit of God may talk about the love of Christ, he may write poetry about it, he may give speeches about it, but it is only words, words, words. There is no real apprehension. But the Spirit of God makes us strong to really apprehend it in all its breadth, in all its length, in all its depth, and in all its height.

4. *In our being "filled to the measure of all the fullness of God."*

One older translation reads "Filled WITH all the fullness of God." Later translations more accurately translated this "filled *unto*" or "filled *to*" the fullness of God. To be filled WITH all the fullness of God would not be so wonderful, for it is an easy matter to fill a 2-Liter bottle with all the fullness of the ocean, a single dip will do it. But it would be an impossibility indeed to fill a 2-Liter bottle UNTO all the fullness of the ocean, until all the fullness that there is in the ocean is in that 2-Liter bottle. But it is seemingly a more impossible task that the Holy Spirit undertakes to do for us, to fill us "to the measure of all the fullness" of the infinite God, to fill us until all the intellectual and moral fullness that there is in God is in us. But this is the believer's destiny, we are "heirs of God and co-heirs with Christ" (Romans 8:17), *i. e.*, we are heirs of God to the extent that Jesus Christ is an heir of God; that is, we are heirs to all God is and all God has. It is the work of the Holy Spirit to apply to us that which is already ours in Christ. It is His work to make ours experimentally all God has and all God is, until the work is consummated in our being "FILLED TO THE MEASURE OF ALL THE FULLNESS OF GOD." This is not the work of a moment, nor a day, nor a week, nor a month, nor a year, but the Holy Spirit day by day puts His hand, as it were, into the fullness of God and conveys to us what He has taken from there and puts it into us, and then again He puts His hand into the fullness that there is in God and conveys to us what is taken from there, and puts it into us, and this wonderful process goes on day after day and week after week and month after month, and year after year, and never ends until we are "filled TO the measure of all the fullness of God."

CHAPTER 10: THE HOLY SPIRIT AND SONSHIP

1. *The Holy Spirit leads the believer into life as a son.*

> *...those who are led by the Spirit of God are sons of God.* – Romans 8:14

In this passage we see the Holy Spirit taking the conduct of the believer's life. A true Christian life is a personally conducted life, conducted at every turn by a Divine Person. It is the believer's privilege to be absolutely set free from all care and worry and anxiety as to the decisions which we must make at any turn of life. The Holy Spirit undertakes all that responsibility for us. A true Christian life is not one governed by a long set of external rules, but led by a living and ever-present Person within us. It is in this connection that Paul says:

> *For you did not receive a spirit that makes you a slave again to fear.* – Romans 8:15a

A life governed by external rules is a life of slavery. There is always FEAR that we haven't come up with quite enough rules, and always the fear that in an unguarded moment we may have broken some of the rules we have made. The life that many professed Christians lead is one of awful bondage; for they have put upon themselves a yoke more grievous to bear than that of the ancient Mosaic law concerning which Peter said to the Jews of his time, that neither they nor their fathers had been able to bear it (Acts 15:10). Many Christians have a long list of self-made rules, "Thou shalt do this," and "Thou shalt do this," and "Thou shalt do this," and "Thou shalt not do that," and "Thou shalt not do that," and "Thou shalt not do that"; and if by any chance they break one of these self-made rules, or forget to keep one of them, they are at once filled with an awful dread that they have brought upon themselves the displeasure of God (and they even sometimes think that they have committed the unpardonable sin). This is not Christianity, this is legalism. *"You did not receive a spirit that makes you a slave again to fear,"* we have received the Spirit who gives us the place of sons:

For you did not receive a spirit that makes you a slave again to fear, <u>but you received the Spirit of sonship</u>. And by him we cry, "Abba, Father." – Romans 8:15

Our lives should not be governed by a set of external rules but by the loving Spirit of Adoption within us. We should believe the teaching of God's Word that the Spirit of God's Son dwells within us and we should surrender the absolute control of our life to Him and look to Him to guide us at every turn of life. He will do it if we only surrender to Him to do it and trust Him to do it. If in a moment of thoughtlessness, we go our own way instead of His, we will not be filled with an overwhelming sense of condemnation and of fear of an offended God, but we will go to God as our Father, confess our going astray, believe that He forgives us fully because He says so (1 John 1:9) and go on living in a desire to obey Him and be led by His Spirit.

Being led by the Spirit of God does not mean for a moment that we will do things that the written Word of God tells us not to do. The Holy Spirit never leads men contrary to the Book of which He Himself is the Author. And if there is some spirit which is leading us to do something that is contrary to the explicit teachings of Jesus, or the Apostles, we may be perfectly sure that this spirit who is leading us is not the Holy Spirit. This point needs to be emphasized in our day, for unfortunately there are many who give themselves over to the leading of some spirit, whom they say is the Holy Spirit, but who is leading them to do things explicitly forbidden in the Word. We must always remember that many false spirits and false prophets have gone out into the world (1 John 4:1). There are many who are so anxious to be led by some unseen power that they are ready to surrender the conduct of their lives to any spiritual influence or unseen person. In this way, they open their lives to the conduct and malevolent influence of evil spirits to the utter wreck and ruin of their lives.

Many professed Christians seek to justify themselves in doing things which are explicitly forbidden in the Word by saying that they are led by the Spirit of God. But the Holy Spirit never contradicts Himself. He never leads the individual to do that which in the written Word He has commanded us not to do. Any leading of the

Spirit must be tested by that which we know to be the leading of the Spirit in the Word. But while we need to be on our guard against the leading of false spirits, it is our privilege to be led by the Holy Spirit, and to lead a life free from the bondage of rules and free from the anxiety that we will not go wrong, a life as children whose Father has sent an unerring Guide to lead them all the way.

Those who are led by the Spirit of God are "SONS of God," that is, they are not merely CHILDREN of God, born of the Father, but immature – they are the grown children, the mature children of God; they are no longer babes but sons.

2. *The Holy Spirit testifies to our sonship.*

One of the most precious passages in the Bible regarding the work of the Holy Spirit is found in Romans 8:15-16:

For you did not receive a spirit that makes you a slave again to fear, but you received the Spirit of sonship. And by him we cry, "Abba, Father." The Spirit himself testifies with our spirit that we are God's children. – Romans 8:15-16

There are two witnesses to our sonship, first, our own spirit, taking God at His Word (John 1:12), bears witness to our sonship. Our own spirit unhesitatingly affirms that what God says is true that we are sons of God because God says so. But there is another witness to our sonship, namely, the Holy Spirit. He testifies WITH our spirit. "With" is the force of the Greek used in this passage. It does not say that He bears witness TO our spirit but *with* it. How He does this is explained in Galatians 4:6:

Because you are sons, God sent the Spirit of his Son into our hearts, the Spirit who calls out, "Abba, Father." – Galatians 4:6

When we have received Jesus Christ as our Savior and accepted God's testimony concerning Christ that through Him we have become sons, the Spirit of His Son comes into our hearts filling them with an overwhelming sense of sonship, and crying through our hearts, "Abba, Father." The natural attitude of our hearts towards God is not that of sons. We may call Him Father with our lips, as when for example we repeat in a formal way, the prayer that Jesus taught us, "Our Father, which art in heaven," but there is no real sense that He is our Father. Our calling Him so is mere words. We do not really trust Him. We do not love to come into His presence; we do not love to look up into His face with a sense of wonderful joy and trust because we are talking to our Father. We dread God. We come to Him in prayer because we think we ought to and perhaps we are afraid of what might happen if we did not. But when the Spirit of His Son bears witness together with our spirit to our sonship, then we are filled and thrilled with the sense that we are sons. We trust Him as we never even trusted our earthly Father. There is even less fear of Him than there was of our earthly father. Reverence there is, awe, but oh such a sense of wonderful childlike trust.

Notice when it is that the Spirit testifies with our spirit that we are the children of God. We have the order of experience in the order of the verses in Romans 8. First we see the Holy Spirit setting us free from the law of sin and death, and consequently, the righteousness of the law fulfilled in us who walk not after the law but after the Spirit (vv. 2-4); then we have the believer not minding the things of the flesh but the things of the Spirit (v. 5); then we have the believer day by day through the Spirit putting to death the deeds of the body (v. 13); then we have the believer led by the Spirit of God; then and only then, we have the Spirit bearing witness to our sonship. There are many seeking the witness of the Spirit to their sonship in the wrong place. They practically demand the witness of the Spirit to their sonship before they have even confessed their acceptance of Christ, and certainly before they have surrendered their lives fully to the control of the indwelling Spirit of God. No, let us seek things in their right order. Let us accept Jesus Christ as our Savior, and surrender to Him as our Lord and Master, because God commands us to do so; let us confess Him before the world because God commands that (Matthew 10:32-33; Romans 10:9-10); let us assert that our sins are forgiven, that we have eternal life, that we are sons of God because God says so in His Word and we are unwilling to make God a liar by doubting Him (Acts 10:43; 13:38-39; 1 John 5:10-13; John 5:24; John 1:12); let us surrender our lives to the control of the Spirit of Life, looking to Him to set us free from the law of sin and death; let us set our minds, not upon the things of the flesh but the things of the Spirit; let us through the Spirit day by day put to death the deeds of the body; let us give our lives up to be led by the Spirit of God in all things; and THEN let us simply trust God to send the Spirit of His Son into our hearts filling us with a sense of sonship, crying, "Abba, Father," and He will do it.

God, our Father, longs that we will know and realize that we are His sons. He longs to hear us call Him Father from hearts that realize what they say, and that trust Him without a fear or anxiety. He is our Father, He alone in all the universe realizes the fullness of meaning that there is in that wonderful word "Father," and it brings joy to Him to have us realize that He is our Father and to address Him in this way.

There is a Father who loves as no earthly father, who longs to have His children realize that they are children, and when we look up into His face and from a heart which the Holy Spirit has filled with a sense of sonship call Him "Abba" (papa), "Father." No language can describe the joy of God.

CHAPTER 11: THE HOLY SPIRIT AS TEACHER

Our Lord Jesus in His last conversation with His disciples before His crucifixion said:

> *But the Counselor, the Holy Spirit, whom the Father will send in my name, will teach you all things and will remind you of everything I have said to you.* – John 14:26

Here we have a twofold work of the Holy Spirit, teaching and bringing to remembrance the things which Christ had already taught. We will consider them in the reverse order.

1. *The Holy Spirit brings to remembrance the words of Christ.*

This promise was made primarily to the Apostles and is the guarantee of the accuracy of their report of what Jesus said; but the Holy Spirit does a similar work with each believer who expects it of Him, and who looks to Him to do it. The Holy Spirit brings to our mind the teachings of Christ and of the Word just when we need them for either the necessities of our life or of our service. Many of us could tell of occasions when we were in great distress of soul or great questioning as to duty or great extremity as to what to say to one whom we were trying to lead to Christ or to help, and at that exact moment the very Scripture we needed—some passage it may be we had not thought of for a long time and quite likely of which we had never thought in this connection—was brought to mind. Who did it? The Holy Spirit did it. He is ready to do it even more frequently, if we only expect it of Him and look to Him to do it. It is our privilege every time we sit down beside an inquirer to point him to the way of life to look up to the Holy Spirit and say, "Just what shall I say to this inquirer? Just what Scripture shall I use?" There is a deep significance in the fact that in the verse immediately following this precious promise Jesus says, "Peace I leave with you, My peace I give unto you." It is by the Spirit bringing His words to remembrance and teaching us the truth of God that we obtain and abide in this peace. If we will simply look to the Holy Spirit to bring to mind Scripture just when we need it, and just the Scripture we need, we will indeed have Christ's peace every moment of our lives.

2. *The Holy Spirit will teach us all things.*

There is a still more explicit promise to this effect two chapters further on in John:

> *"I have much more to say to you, more than you can now bear. But when he, the Spirit of truth, comes, he will guide you into all truth. He will not speak on his own; he will speak only what he hears, and he will tell you what is yet to come. He will bring glory to me by taking from what is mine and making it known to you."* – John 16:12-14

This promise was made in the first instance to the Apostles, but the Apostles themselves applied it to all believers (1 John 2:20, 27).

It is the privilege of each believer in Jesus Christ, even the humblest, to be taught of God. Each humblest believer is independent of human teachers:

> *As for you, the anointing you received from him remains in you, and you do not need anyone to teach you. But as his anointing teaches you about all things and as that anointing is real, not counterfeit--just as it has taught you, remain in him.* – 1 John 2:27

This, of course, does not mean that we may not learn much from others who are taught of the Holy Spirit. If John had thought that he would never have written this epistle to teach others. The man who is the most fully taught of God is the very one who will be most ready to listen to what God has taught others. Much less does it mean that when we are taught of the Spirit, we are independent of the written Word of God; for the Word is the very place to which the Spirit, who is the Author of the Word, leads His pupils and the instrument through which He instructs them (Ephesians 6:17; John 6:33; Ephesians 5:18-19; Colossians 3:16). But while we may learn much from men, we are not dependent upon them. We have a Divine Teacher, the Holy Spirit.

We shall never truly know the truth until we are taught directly by the Holy Spirit. No amount of mere human teaching, no matter who our teachers may be, will ever give us a correct and exact and full apprehension of the truth. Not even a diligent study of the Word either in the English or in the original languages will give us a real understanding of the truth. Each one of us must be taught directly by the Holy Spirit. The one who is taught by Him will understand the truth of God better even if he does not know one word of Greek or Hebrew, than the one who knows Greek and Hebrew thoroughly and all the cognate languages as well, but who is not taught of the Spirit.

The Spirit will guide the one whom He teaches "into all the truth." The whole sphere of God's truth is for each one of us, but the Holy Spirit will not guide us into all the truth in a single day, nor in a week, nor in a year, but step by step. There are two specific lines of the Spirit's teaching mentioned:

> 1) "He will tell you what is yet to come" (John 16:13b)

There are many who say we can know nothing of the future, that all our thoughts on that subject are guesswork. It is true that we cannot know everything about the future. There are some things which God has seen fit to keep to Himself, secret things which belong to Him (Deut. 29:29). For example, we cannot "know the times or dates" of our Lord's return (Acts 1:7), but there are many things about the future which the Holy Spirit will reveal to us.

> 2) "He will bring glory to me (i.e. Christ) by taking from what is mine and making it known to you." (John 16:14)

This is the Holy Spirit's specific line of teaching with the believer, as with the unbeliever, Jesus Christ. It is His work above all else to reveal Jesus Christ and to glorify Him. His whole teaching centers in Christ. From one point of view or the other, He is always bringing us to Jesus Christ. There are some who fear to emphasize the truth about the Holy Spirit lest Christ Himself be disparaged and put in the background, but there is no one who magnifies Christ as the Holy Spirit does. We shall never understand Christ, nor see His glory until the Holy Spirit interprets Him to us. No amount of listening to sermons and lectures, no matter how great they might be, no amount of mere study of the Word even, would ever give us to see the things of Christ; the Holy Spirit must show us and He is willing to do it and He can do it. He is longing to do it. The Holy Spirit's most intense desire is to reveal Jesus Christ to men. On the day of Pentecost when Peter and the rest of the company were "filled with the Holy Spirit," they did not talk much about the Holy Spirit, they talked about Christ. Study Peter's sermon on that day; Jesus Christ was his one theme, and Jesus Christ will be our one theme, if we are taught of the Spirit; Jesus Christ will occupy the whole horizon of our vision. We will have a new Christ, a glorious Christ. Christ will be so glorious to us that we will long to go and tell every one about this glorious One whom we have found. Jesus Christ is so different when the Spirit glorifies Him by taking of His things and showing them to us.

3. *The Holy Spirit reveals to us the deep things of God which are hidden from and are foolishness to the natural man.*

> *However, as it is written: "No eye has seen, no ear has heard, no mind has conceived what God has prepared for those who love him" -- but God has revealed it to us by his Spirit. The Spirit searches all things, even the deep things of God. For who among men knows the thoughts of a man except the man's spirit within him? In the same way no one knows the thoughts of God except the Spirit of God. We have not received the spirit of the world but the Spirit who is from God, that we may understand what God has freely given us. This is what we speak, not in words taught us by human wisdom but in words taught by the Spirit, expressing spiritual truths in spiritual words.* – 1 Corinthians 2:9-13

This passage, of course, refers primarily to the Apostles but we cannot limit this work of the Spirit to them. The Spirit reveals to the individual believer the deep things of God, things which human eye has not seen, nor ear heard, things which have not entered into the heart of man, the things which God has prepared for them that love Him. It is evident from the context that this does not refer solely to heaven, or the things to come in the life hereafter. The Holy Spirit takes the deep things of God which God has prepared for us, even in the life that now is, and reveals them to us.

4. *The Holy Spirit interprets His own revelation. He imparts power to discern, know and appreciate what He has taught.*

In the next verse to those just quoted we read:

The man without the Spirit does not accept the things that come from the Spirit of God, for they are foolishness to him, and he cannot understand them, because they are spiritually discerned. – 1 Corinthians 2:14

Not only is the Holy Spirit the Author of revelation, the written Word of God: He is also the Interpreter of what He has revealed. Any profound book is immeasurably more interesting and helpful when we have the author of the book right at hand to interpret it to us, and it is always our privilege to have the author of the Bible right at hand when we study it. The Holy Spirit is the Author of the Bible and He stands ready to interpret its meaning to every believer every time he opens the Book. To understand the Book, we must look to Him, then the darkest places become clear. We often need to pray with the Psalmist of old:

Open my eyes that I may see wonderful things in your law. – Psalms 119:18

It is not enough that we have the revelation of God before us in the written Word to study, we must also have the inward illumination of the Holy Spirit to enable us to apprehend it as we study. It is a common mistake, but a most palpable mistake, to try to comprehend a spiritual revelation with the natural understanding. It is the foolish attempt to do this that has landed so many in the bog of so-called "Higher Criticism." In order to understand art a man must have æsthetic sense as well as the knowledge of colors and of paint, and a man to understand a spiritual revelation must be taught of the Spirit. A mere knowledge of the languages in which the Bible was written is not enough. A man with no æsthetic sense might as well expect to appreciate the Sistine Madonna, because he is not color blind, as a man who is not filled with the Spirit to understand the Bible, simply because he understands the vocabulary and the laws of grammar of the languages in which the Bible was written. We might as well think of setting a man to teach art because he understood paints as to set a man to teach the Bible because he has a thorough understanding of Greek and Hebrew. In our day we need not only to recognize the utter insufficiency and worthlessness before God of our own righteousness, which is the lesson of the opening chapters of the Epistle to the Romans, but also the utter insufficiency and worthlessness in the things of God of our own wisdom, which is the lesson of the First Epistle to the Corinthians, especially the first to the third chapters. (See for example 1 Corinthians 1:19-21, 26-27.)

The Jews of old had a revelation by the Spirit but they failed to depend upon the Spirit Himself to interpret it to them, so they went astray. So Christians today have a revelation by the Spirit and many are failing to depend upon the Holy Spirit to interpret it to them and so they go astray. The whole evangelical church recognizes theoretically at least the utter insufficiency of man's own righteousness. What it needs to be taught in the present hour, and what it needs to be made to feel, is the utter insufficiency of man's wisdom. That is perhaps the lesson which this twenty-first century of towering intellectual conceit needs most of any to learn. To understand God's Word, we must empty ourselves utterly of our own wisdom and rest in utter dependence upon the Spirit of God to interpret it to us. We do well to lay to heart the words of Jesus Himself:

> *At that time Jesus said, "I praise you, Father, Lord of heaven and earth, because you have hidden these things from the wise and learned, and revealed them to little children." –* Matthew 11:25

A number of Bible students were once discussing the best methods of Bible study and one man, who was in point of fact a learned and scholarly man, said, "I think the best method of Bible study is the baby method." When we have entirely put away our own righteousness, then and only then, we get the righteousness of God (Phil. 3:4-7, 9; Romans 10:3). And when we have entirely put away our own wisdom, then, and only then, we get the wisdom of God.

> *Do not deceive yourselves. If any one of you thinks he is wise by the standards of this age, he should become a "fool" so that he may become wise. –* 1 Corinthians 3:18

The emptying must precede filling, the self poured out that God may be poured in. We must daily be taught by the Spirit to understand the Word. We cannot depend today on the fact that the Spirit taught us yesterday. Each new time that we come in contact with the Word, it must be in the power of the Spirit for that specific occasion. That the Holy Spirit once illumined our mind to grasp a certain truth is not enough. He must do it each time we confront that passage.

5. *The Holy Spirit enables the believer to communicate to others in power the truth he himself has been taught.*

> *When I came to you, brothers, I did not come with eloquence or superior wisdom as I proclaimed to you the testimony about God. For I resolved to know nothing while I was with you except Jesus Christ and him crucified. I came to you in weakness and fear, and with much trembling. My message and my preaching were not with wise and persuasive words, but with a demonstration of the Spirit's power, so that your faith might not rest on men's wisdom, but on God's power. –* 1 Corinthians 2:1-5

> *Because our gospel came to you not simply with words, but also with power, with the Holy Spirit and with deep conviction. You know how we lived among you for your sake. –* 1 Thessalonians 1:5

We need not only the Holy Spirit to reveal the truth to chosen apostles and prophets in the first place, and the Holy Spirit in the second place to interpret to us as individuals the truth He has revealed, but in the third place, we need the Holy Spirit to enable us to effectually communicate to others the truth which He Himself has interpreted to us. We need Him all along the line. One great cause of real failure in the ministry, even when there is seeming success, and not only in the regular ministry but in all forms of service as well, comes from the attempt to teach by enticing words of man's wisdom (that is, by the arts of human logic, rhetoric, persuasion and eloquence) what the Holy Spirit has taught us. What is needed is Holy Spirit power, "a *demonstration of the Spirit's power.*" There are three causes of failure in preaching today. First, Some other message is taught than the message which the Holy Spirit has revealed in the

Word. (Men preach science, art, literature, philosophy, sociology, history, economics, experience, etc., and not the simple Word of God as found in the Holy Spirit's Book,—the Bible.) Second, The Spirit-taught message of the Bible is studied and sought to be apprehended by the natural understanding, that is, without the Spirit's illumination. How common that is, even in institutions where men are being trained for the ministry, even institutions which may be altogether orthodox. Third, The Spirit-given message, the Word, the Bible studied and apprehended under the Holy Ghost's illumination is given out to others with enticing words of man's wisdom, and not in "a *demonstration of the Spirit's power.*" We need, and we are absolutely dependent upon the Spirit all along the line. He must teach us how to speak as well as what to speak. His must be the power as well as the message.

CHAPTER 12: PRAYING, RETURNING THANKS, AND WORSHIPING IN THE HOLY SPIRIT

Two of the most deeply significant passages in the Bible on the subject of the Holy Spirit and on the subject of prayer are found in Jude 20 and Ephesians 6:18:

But you, dear friends, build yourselves up in your most holy faith and pray in the Holy Spirit. – Jude 20

And pray in the Spirit on all occasions with all kinds of prayers and requests. With this in mind, be alert and always keep on praying for all the saints. – Ephesians 6:18

1. *The Holy Spirit guides the believer in prayer.*

The disciples did not know how to pray as they ought so they came to Jesus and said, "Lord, teach us to pray" (Luke 11:1). We today do not know how to pray as we ought—we do not know what to pray for, nor how to ask for it—but there is One who is always at hand to help (John 14:16-17) and He knows what we should pray for. He helps our infirmity in this matter of prayer as in other matters (Romans 8:26). He teaches us to pray. True prayer is prayer in the Spirit (*i. e.*, the prayer that the Holy Spirit inspires and directs). The prayer in which the Holy Spirit leads us is the prayer "in accordance with God's will" (Romans 8:27). When we ask anything according to God's will, we know that He hears us and we know that He has granted the things that we ask (1 John 5:14-15). We may know it is ours at the moment when we pray just as surely as we know it afterwards when we have it in our actual possession. But how can we know the will of God when we pray? By what is written in His Word; all the promises in the Bible are sure and if God promises anything in the Bible, we may be sure it is His will to give us that thing; but there are many things that we need which are not specifically promised in the Word and still even in that case it is our privilege to know the will of God, for it is the work of the Holy Spirit to teach us God's will and lead us out in prayer along the line of God's will. Some object to the Christian doctrine of prayer; for they say that it teaches that we can go to God in our ignorance and change His will and subject His infinite wisdom to our erring foolishness. But that is not the Christian doctrine of prayer at all; the Christian doctrine of prayer is that it is the believer's privilege to be taught by the Spirit of God Himself to know what the will of God is and not to ask for the things that our foolishness would prompt us to ask for but to ask for things that the never-erring Spirit of God prompts us to ask for. True prayer is prayer "in the Spirit," that is, the prayer which the Spirit inspires and directs. When we come into God's presence, we should recognize our infirmity, our ignorance of what is best for us, our ignorance of what we should pray for, our ignorance of how we should pray for it and in the consciousness of our utter inability to pray in the right way look up to the Holy Spirit to teach us to pray, and cast ourselves utterly upon Him to direct our prayers and to lead out our desires and guide our utterance of them. Rushing heedlessly into God's presence and asking the first thing that comes into our minds, or that some other thoughtless person asks us to pray for, is not praying "in the Holy Spirit" and is not true prayer. The prayer that God, the Holy Spirit, inspires is the prayer that God, the Father, answers.

The longings which the Holy Spirit places in our hearts are often too deep for utterance, too deep apparently for clear and definite comprehension on the part of the believer himself in whom the Spirit is working:

> *In the same way, the Spirit helps us in our weakness. We do not know what we ought to pray for, but the Spirit himself intercedes for us with groans that words cannot express.* – Romans 8:26

God Himself must search the heart to know what is the mind of the Spirit in these unuttered and unutterable longings. But God does know what is the mind of the Spirit; He does know what these Spirit-given longings which we cannot put into words mean, even if we do not, and these longings are according to the will of God, and God grants them. It is in this way that it comes to pass that God is able to do exceedingly abundantly above all that we ask or think, according to the power that works within us (Ephesians 3:20). There are other times when the Spirit's leadings are so clear that we pray with the Spirit and with the understanding also (1 Corinthians 14:15). We distinctly understand what it is that the Holy Spirit leads us to pray for.

2. *The Holy Spirit inspires the believer and guides him in thanksgiving.*

> *Do not get drunk on wine, which leads to debauchery. Instead, be filled with the Spirit. Speak to one another with psalms, hymns and spiritual songs. Sing and make music in your heart to the Lord, <u>always giving thanks</u> to God the Father for everything, in the name of our Lord Jesus Christ.* – Ephesians 5:18-20

Not only does the Holy Spirit teach us to pray, He also teaches us to give thanks. One of the most prominent characteristics of the Spirit-filled life is thanksgiving. On the Day of Pentecost, when the disciples were filled with the Holy Spirit, and spoke as the Spirit enabled them, we hear them telling the wonderful works of God (Acts 2:4, 11), and today when any believer is filled with the Holy Spirit, he always becomes filled with thanksgiving and praise. True thanksgiving is "TO God the Father," "*in* the name of" our Lord Jesus Christ, IN the Holy Spirit.

3. *The Holy Spirit inspires worship on the part of the believer.*

> *For it is we who are the circumcision, we <u>who worship by the Spirit of God</u>, who glory in Christ Jesus, and who put no confidence in the flesh.* – Philippians 3:3

Prayer is not worship; thanksgiving is not worship. Worship is a definite act of the creature in relation to God. Worship is bowing before God in adoring acknowledgment and contemplation of Himself and the perfection of His being. Someone has said, "In our prayers, we are taken up with our needs; in our thanksgiving we are taken up with our blessings; in our worship, we are taken up with Himself." There is no true and acceptable worship except that which the Holy Spirit prompts and directs.

"Yet a time is coming and has now come when the true worshipers will worship the Father in spirit and truth, for they are the kind of worshipers the Father seeks. God is spirit, and his worshipers must worship in spirit and in truth." – John 4:23-24

The flesh seeks to intrude into every sphere of life. The flesh has its worship as well as its lusts. The worship which the flesh prompts is an abomination unto God. In this we see the folly of any attempt at a gathering of religions where the representatives of radically different religions attempt to worship together.

Not all earnest and honest worship is worship in the Spirit. A man may be very honest and very earnest in his worship and still not have submitted himself to the guidance of the Holy Spirit in the matter and so his worship is in the flesh. Oftentimes even when there is great loyalty to the letter of the Word, worship may not be "in the Spirit," *i. e.*, inspired and directed by Him. To worship the way God desires, we must have "no confidence in the flesh," (Phil. 3:3) that is, we must recognize the utter inability of the flesh (our natural self as contrasted to the Divine Spirit that dwells in and should mold everything in the believer) to worship acceptably. And we must also realize the danger that the flesh will intrude itself into our worship. In utter self-distrust we must cast ourselves upon the Holy Spirit to lead us to the right direction in our worship. Just as we must renounce any merit in ourselves and cast ourselves upon Christ and His work for us upon the cross for justification, just so we must renounce any supposed capacity for good in ourselves and cast ourselves utterly upon the Holy Spirit and His work in us, in holy living, knowing, praying, thanking and WORSHIPPING and all else that we are to do.

CHAPTER 13: THE HOLY SPIRIT SENDING PEOPLE OUT TO DO WORKS OF SERVICE

While they were worshiping the Lord and fasting, the Holy Spirit said, "<u>Set apart for me</u> Barnabas and Saul for the work to which I have called them." So after they had fasted and prayed, they placed their hands on them and sent them off. The two of them, <u>sent on their way by the Holy Spirit</u>, went down to Seleucia and sailed from there to Cyprus. – Acts 13:2-4

It is evident from this passage that THE HOLY SPIRIT CALLS MEN INTO DEFINITE LINES OF WORK AND SENDS THEM FORTH INTO THE WORK. He not only calls men in a general way into Christian work, but selects the specific work and points it out. Many people ask, "Should I go to Haiti, to Africa, to India?" There is only one Person who can rightly settle that question for you and that Person is the Holy Spirit. You cannot settle the question for yourself, much less can any other man settle it rightly for you. Not every Christian man is called to go to Haiti; not every Christian woman is called to go to Africa; not every Christian man is called to go to the foreign field at all. God alone knows whether He wants you in any of these places, but He is willing to show you. In a day such as we live in, when there is such a need of the right men and the right women on the foreign field, every young and healthy and intellectually competent Christian man and woman should definitely offer themselves to God for the foreign field and ask Him if He wants them to go. But they should not to go until He, by His Holy Spirit, makes it plain.

The great need in all lines of Christian work today is men and women whom the Holy Ghost calls and sends forth. We have plenty of men and women whom men have called and sent forth. We have plenty of men and women who have called themselves, for there are many today who object strenuously to being sent forth by men, by any organization of any kind, but, in fact, are what is immeasurably worse, sent forth by themselves and not by God.

1. *How does the Holy Spirit call?*

The passage before us does not tell us how the Holy Spirit spoke to the group of prophets and teachers in Antioch, telling them to separate Barnabas and Saul to the work to which He had called them. It is presumably purposely silent on this point. Possibly it is silent on this point so that we should not think that the Holy Spirit must always call in precisely the same way. There is nothing whatever to indicate that He spoke by an audible voice, much less is there anything to indicate that He made His will known in any of the fantastic ways in which some in these days profess to discern His leading—as for example, by twitchings of the body, by shuddering, by opening of the Bible at random and putting his finger on a passage that may be construed into some entirely different meaning than that which the inspired author intended by it. The important point is, He made His will clearly known, and He is willing to make His will clearly known to us today. Sometimes He makes it known in one way and sometimes in another, but He will make it known.

2. *How can we receive the Holy Spirit's call?*

First of all, by desiring it; second, by earnestly seeking it; third, by waiting upon the Lord for it; fourth, by expecting it. The record reads, *"While they were worshiping the Lord and fasting."* They were waiting upon the Lord for His direction. For the time being they had turned their back utterly upon worldly cares and desires, even upon those things which were perfectly proper in their place. Many a man is saying today in justification for his staying home from the foreign field, "I have never had a call." But how do you know that? Have you been listening for a call? God usually speaks in a still small voice and it is only the listening ear that can catch it. Have you ever definitely offered yourself to God to send you where He will? While no man or woman ought to go to India or Africa or other foreign field unless they are clearly and definitely called, they ought to each offer themselves to God for this work and be ready for the call and be listening sharply that they may hear the call if it comes. Let it be borne distinctly in mind that a man needs no more definite call to Africa than to Boston, or New York, or London, or any other desirable field at home.

The Holy Spirit not only calls men and sends them forth into definite lines of work, but He also GUIDES IN THE DETAILS OF DAILY LIFE AND SERVICE AS TO WHERE TO GO AND WHERE NOT TO GO, WHAT TO DO AND WHAT NOT TO DO.

> *So he started out, and on his way he met an Ethiopian eunuch, an important official in charge of all the treasury of Candace, queen of the Ethiopians. This man had gone to Jerusalem to worship, and on his way home was sitting in his chariot reading the book of Isaiah the prophet. The Spirit told Philip, "Go to that chariot and stay near it." – Acts 8:27-29*

Here we see the Spirit guiding Philip in the details of service into which He had called him. In a similar way, we read in Acts 16:6-7:

> *Paul and his companions traveled throughout the region of Phrygia and Galatia, having been kept by the Holy Spirit from preaching the word in the province of Asia. When they came to the border of Mysia, they tried to enter Bithynia, but the Spirit of Jesus would not allow them to. – Acts 16:6-7*

Here we see the Holy Spirit directing Paul where not to go. It is possible for us to have the unerring guidance of the Holy Spirit at every turn of life. Take, for example, our personal work. It is manifestly not God's intention that we speak to every one we meet. To attempt to do so would be to attempt the impossible, and we would waste much time in trying to speak to people where we could do no good that might be used in speaking to people where we could accomplish something. There are some to whom it would be wise for us to speak. There are others to whom it would be unwise for us to speak. Time spent on them would be taken from work that would be more to God's glory. Doubtless as Philip journeyed towards Gaza, he met many before he met the one of whom the Spirit said, *"Go to that chariot and stay near it."* The Spirit is as ready to guide us as He was to guide Philip. He is ready to guide us, not only in our more definite forms of Christian work but in all the affairs of life, business, study, everything we have to do. There is no promise in the Bible more plainly explicit than James 1:5-7:

If any of you lacks wisdom, he should ask God, who gives generously to all without finding fault, and it will be given to him. But when he asks, he must believe and not doubt, because he who doubts is like a wave of the sea, blown and tossed by the wind. That man should not think he will receive anything from the Lord. – James 1:5-7

This passage not only promises God's wisdom but tells us specifically just what to do to obtain it. There are really five steps stated or implied in the passage:

  1) We lack wisdom.

We must be conscious of and fully admit our own inability to decide wisely. Here is where oftentimes we fail to receive God's wisdom. We think we are able to decide for ourselves or at least we are not ready to admit our own utter inability to decide. There must be an entire renunciation of the wisdom of the flesh.

  2) We must really desire to know God's way and be willing at any cost to do God's will.

This is implied in the word "ASK." The asking must be sincere, and if we are not willing to do God's will, whatever it may be, at any cost, the asking is not sincere. This is a point of fundamental importance. There is nothing that goes so far to make our minds clear in the discernment of the will of God as revealed by His Spirit as an absolutely surrendered will. Here we find the reason why men oftentimes do not know God's will and have the Spirit's guidance. They are not willing to do whatever the Spirit leads at any cost. It is he that *"chooses to do God's will"* (John 7:17) who shall know, not only of the doctrine, but he shall know his daily duty. Men oftentimes say, "I cannot find out the will of God," but when they are asked the question, "Are you willing to do the will of God at any cost?" they admit that they are not. The way that is very obscure when we hold back from an absolute surrender to God becomes as clear as day when we make that surrender.

  3) We must definitely "ask" guidance.

It is not enough to desire; it is not enough to be willing to obey; we must ASK, definitely ask, God to show us the way.

4) We must confidently expect guidance.

"When he asks, he must believe and not doubt." There are many who cannot find the way, though they ask God to show it to them, simply because they do not have the absolutely undoubting expectation that God will show them the way. God promises to show it if we expect it confidently. When you come to God in prayer to show you what to do, know for a certainty that He will show you. In what way He will show you, He does not tell, but He promises that He will show you and that is enough.

5) We must follow step by step as the guidance comes.

As said before, just how it will come, no one can tell, but it will come. Oftentimes only a step will be made clear at a time; that is all we need to know—the next step. Many are in darkness because they do not know and cannot find what God would have them do next week, or next month or next year. God delights to lead His children a step at a time. He leads us as He led the children of Israel.

Whenever the cloud lifted from above the Tent, the Israelites set out; wherever the cloud settled, the Israelites encamped. At the LORD's command the Israelites set out, and at his command they encamped. As long as the cloud stayed over the tabernacle, they remained in camp. When the cloud remained over the tabernacle a long time, the Israelites obeyed the LORD's order and did not set out. Sometimes the cloud was over the tabernacle only a few days; at the LORD's command they would encamp, and then at his command they would set out. Sometimes the cloud stayed only from evening till morning, and when it lifted in the morning, they set out. Whether by day or by night, whenever the cloud lifted, they set out. Whether the cloud stayed over the tabernacle for two days or a month or a year, the Israelites would remain in camp and not set out; but when it lifted, they would set out. At the LORD's command they encamped, and at the LORD's command they set out. They obeyed the LORD's order, in accordance with his command through Moses. – Numbers 9:17-23

Many who have given themselves up to the leading of the Holy Spirit get into a place of great bondage and are tortured because they have leadings which they fear may be from God but they are not sure. If they do not obey these leadings, they are fearful they have disobeyed God and sometimes believe that they have grieved the Holy Spirit because they did not follow His leading. This is all unnecessary. Let us settle it in our minds that God's guidance is CLEAR guidance.

This is the message we have heard from him and declare to you: God is light; in him there is no darkness at all. – 1 John 1:5

Any leading that is not perfectly clear is not from Him. That is, if our wills are absolutely surrendered to Him. Of course, the obscurity may arise from an unsurrendered will. But if our wills are absolutely surrendered to God, we have the right as God's children to be sure that any guidance is from Him before we obey it. We have a right to go to our Father and say, "Heavenly Father, here I am. I desire above all things to do Your will. Now make it clear to me, Your child. If this thing that I have a leading to do is Your will, I will do it, but make it clear as day if it be Your will." If it is His will, the heavenly Father will make it as clear as day. And you need not, and ought not to do that thing until He does make it clear, and you need not and ought not to condemn yourself because you did not do it. God does not want His children to be in a state of condemnation before Him. He wishes us to be free from all care, worry, anxiety and self-condemnation. Any earthly parent would make the way clear to his child that asked to know it and how much more will our heavenly Father make it clear to us, and until He does make it clear, we need have no fears that in not doing it, we are disobeying God. We have no right to dictate to God HOW He will give His guidance—as, for example, by asking Him to shut up every way, or by asking Him to give a sign, or by guiding us in putting our finger on a text, or in any other way. It is ours to seek and to expect wisdom but it is not ours to dictate how it shall be given. The Holy Spirit *"gives them to each one, just as <u>he determines</u>"* (1 Corinthians 12:11).

Two things are evident from what has been said about the work of the Holy Spirit. First, how utterly dependent we are upon the work of the Holy Spirit at every turn of Christian life and service. Second, how perfect is the provision for life and service that God has made. How wonderful is the fullness of privilege that is open to the humblest believer through the Holy Spirit's work. It is not so much what we are by nature, either intellectually, morally, physically, or even spiritually, that is important. The important matter is, what the Holy Spirit can do for us and what we will let Him do. Not infrequently, the Holy Spirit takes the one who seems to give the least natural promise and uses him far beyond those who give the greatest natural promise. Christian life is not to be lived in the realm of natural temperament, and Christian work is not to be done in the power of natural endowment, but Christian life is to be lived in the realm of the Spirit, and Christian work is to be done on the power of the Spirit. The Holy Spirit is willing and eagerly desirous of doing for each one of us His whole work, and He will do in each one of us all that we will let Him do.

CHAPTER 14: THE HOLY SPIRIT'S ANOINTING OVER THE INDIVIDUAL CHRISTIAN'S LIFE

Two cows were grazing in a pasture when they saw a milk truck pass. On the side of the truck were the words, "Pasteurized, Homogenized, Standardized, Vitamin A added." One cow sighed and said to the other, "Makes you feel kind of inadequate, doesn't it?"

Maybe you can relate to these poor cows today – you feel inadequate, or lack confidence, or don't feel that you have the skills and talents that others do. You see the superstar athletes, movie stars, famous musicians, and feel that in some way you are inferior to them, or maybe even to the ordinary people that you are around on a regular basis.

I'm here to tell you something today – if you are a Christ Follower, you have nothing to feel inferior about – you have been chosen by God to serve a purpose in this world, and that makes you somebody in the eyes of God.

In the Old Testament the word "anointed" was used in a symbolic way to describe someone chosen by God. The word was normally used for someone God had named as King, a Prophet, or a Priest. In the New Testament the word is used to describe each and every one of us who are Christians.

> *Now it is God who makes both us and you stand firm in Christ. He anointed us, set his seal of ownership on us, and put his Spirit in our hearts as a deposit, guaranteeing what is to come.*
> – 2 Corinthians 1:21-22

There are four specific things in this passage that God has done for us. Each one builds upon the other and are all connected to this idea of anointing.

1. *God has given us the Ability to Stand Firm.*

Runner's World (8/91) told the story of Beth Anne DeCiantis's attempt to qualify for the 1992 Olympic Trials marathon. A female runner has to complete the 26-mile, 385-yard race in less than two hours, 45 minutes to compete at the Olympic Trials. Beth started strong but began having trouble around mile 23. She reached the final straightaway at 2:43, with just two minutes left to qualify. Two hundred yards from the finish, she stumbled and fell. Dazed, she stayed down for twenty seconds. The crowd yelled, "Get up!" The clock was ticking--2:44, less than a minute to go Beth Anne staggered to her feet and began walking. Five yards short of the finish, with 10 seconds to go, she fell again. She began to crawl, the crowd cheering her on, and crossed the finish line on her hands and knees – Her time? Two hours, 44 minutes, 57 seconds. Beth Anne's training and willpower gave her the endurance she needed to finish.

In our walk with Christ we find that we need a similar type of training and willpower to make it through life. We have temptations and struggles trying to pull us away from our faith. And in those times we have to rely on our own resources to pull us through. The time that we spend in the Word and prayer will equip us to withstand. Every moment we spend with the Lord in training will benefit us in giving us strength to overcome the powers that try to knock us off our path. But praise God that through His Spirit He also gives us the ability to stand firm so that we are not facing the struggle alone.

> Now *it is God who makes* both us and *you stand firm in Christ*.
> – 2 Corinthians 1:21

Instead of letting us waver and stumble, God empowers us to keep our commitment to Christ. He is with us to guide us, to encourage us, to strengthen us, and sometimes to rebuke us, so that we will stand firm in our commitment to Christ. While I must work at growing to maturity so that I have the resources necessary to resist opposition to my faith, I must also rely on God as my source to overcome. If I try to do this completely on my own I am bound to fail. If I trust in God to see me through, I can only experience success.

2. *God has Set Us Apart for Service.*

1 Corinthians 1:21 ends with the second thing God has given us – *"(God) anointed us."* As we saw earlier it was customary in the Old Testament to *ANOINT* kings, prophets, and priests, as they began their service as a part of the ceremony of inauguration. They were being consecrated, or set apart, to fulfill the duties of a particular office God had chosen for them. But what we see in the Old Testament is just a shadow of what was to come. These Old Testament shadows anticipated the spiritual anointing that would come on all true believers. All those who are in Christ (who the Bible describes as the Anointed One), are themselves anointed by the Holy Spirit by virtue of their union with Christ. This anointing of the Holy Spirit involves the Spirit's indwelling presence and empowerment.

> *I pray that out of his glorious riches he may strengthen you with power through his Spirit in your inner being* – Ephesians 3:16

> *Now to him who is able to do immeasurably more than all we ask or imagine, according to his power that is at work within us* – Ephesians 3:20

In both of these cases, the Word is telling us that our anointing results in empowerment to accomplish the tasks God sets before us. The Spirit's anointing also empowers us for special service. If God sets you apart as a preacher He will empower you to preach. If God sets you apart as a care-giver He will empower you to show mercy. If God sets you apart as a leader He will empower you to lead.

God anoints us and imparts to us the spiritual gifts necessary to accomplish the tasks that He has set us apart to accomplish. Today God is looking into your heart and mine, knowing whether we are receiving and acting upon the anointing He has given to us. What is your ministry? What has God anointed and gifted you to accomplish? Where are the fruits of your labors? If you are acting upon your anointing, these questions will be easy to answer. If you're not, you are missing out on the opportunity of a lifetime.

3. *God has placed His Seal of Ownership Upon Us.*

Have you ever sent a letter through the Post Office and it never reached its destination? If we want to be sure that a letter is going to arrive at the right place, we have that letter registered. The Post Office puts a seal on it, guaranteeing that they will get the letter to the person to whom it's addressed.

In the days of slavery, it wasn't unusual for a slave owner to mark his slave with a brand, or perhaps a tattoo that was evidence of who the slave belonged to.

All legal documents bear a seal – "In witness thereof I set my seal" is the phraseology that has come down to us from old English.

> *(God has) set his seal of ownership on us* – 2 Corinthians 1:22a

The Holy Spirit has sealed us, branded us, and marked us as His own. He has claimed us as His property. He owns us. The moment we gave our life to Jesus Christ we were marked for all eternity as God's children.

> *And you also were included in Christ when you heard the word of truth, the gospel of your salvation. <u>Having believed, you were marked in him with a seal, the promised Holy Spirit</u>* – Ephesians 1:13

In war we can identify which soldier is from what country, and even which branch of the service he is in, by the uniform that he wears. The same is true when we see opposing teams in sports – they are marked by the color of their uniform and the logo on their clothes. In the motorcycle world, groups of all kinds identify themselves by a patch on their backs.

In a similar way, God can look down at our world and quickly identify which people have given their lives to Him and which ones have not. We are wearing God's uniform when we are indwelt with the Holy Spirit. He identifies us, and acts appropriately toward us based on the seal of ownership He has placed upon us. God promises that we will be safely delivered into His arms when the end of all things takes place.

4. *God has Given Us A Guarantee for the Future.*

(God has) put his Spirit in our hearts as a deposit, guaranteeing what is to come. – 2 Corinthians 1:22b

Now it is God who has made us for this very purpose and has given us the Spirit as a deposit, guaranteeing what is to come. – 2 Corinthians 5:5

When you believed in Christ, he identified you as his own by giving you the Holy Spirit, whom he promised long ago. The Spirit is God's guarantee that he will give us everything he promised and that he has purchased us to be his own people. – Ephesians 1:13b-14a

When you buy a house, you normally have to put down a deposit. And when you put down a deposit that means there is more money that is going to follow. Let's say that you found a house for $100,000 and put $10,000 down on it. You will begin making installment payments until the loan is paid in full.

God has made a deposit in our hearts in the Person of the Holy Spirit. We have the Holy Spirit in our possession, meaning that there is more to come. When we buy something on the installment plan, there is always a possibility that we might back out of the deal, even though we've put a down payment on whatever it is we're purchasing. But there is no backing out of this deal by God. He has purchased us with His blood.

God has put down a deposit, guaranteeing that those of us who are in Christ will be delivered safely into the His hands. Our souls are in escrow, waiting for that final day of redemption. God promises us that our futures are guaranteed and the Holy Spirit who indwells us is evidence that God is going to come through on His promise to us. This also means that this isn't all that we are going to receive in Christ. If we took all of the benefits that we have that come simply from being a Christian that should be enough to satisfy us forever. But God tells us that this is just the beginning – just the first installment of what He has planned for us in the days to come.

CHAPTER 15: THE HOLY SPIRIT GIVES POWER AND GIFTS TO HIS FOLLOWERS

In 1935, Blasio Kugosi, a schoolteacher in Rwanda, Central Africa, was deeply discouraged by the lack of life in the church and the powerlessness of his own experience. He followed the example of the first Christians and closed himself in for a week of prayer and fasting in his little cottage. He emerged a changed man. He confessed his sins to those he had wronged, including his wife and children. He proclaimed the gospel in the school where he taught, and revival broke out there, resulting in students and teachers being saved. They were called *abaka*, meaning "people on fire." Shortly after that, Blasio was invited to Uganda to share with the Anglican Church there. As he called the leaders to repentance, the fire of the Spirit descended again on the place, with similar results as in Rwanda. Several days later, Blasio died of fever. His ministry lasted only a few weeks, but the revival fires sparked through his ministry swept throughout East Africa and continue to the present. Hundreds of thousands of lives have been transformed over the decades through this mighty East African revival. It all began with a discouraged Christian setting himself apart to seek the fullness of God's Spirit.

And that's what it takes in every generation – men and women of God to experience a holy dissatisfaction with the way things are, and with the faith to become everything God wants them to be. There have been great revivals throughout the world since the church began, with many in the United States led by people like Finney, Moody, Torrey and others. But each of these revivals began with a personal revival of the heart, which then spilled over into other people's lives, and the next thing you know, the entire church was on fire with power from on high.

That power for revival and renewal finds its source in one place, and one place only. It comes from the Holy Spirit when we allow ourselves to be filled with His presence. If you are looking for that Holy Spirit power today, I encourage you to listen up, because I want to tell you how to possess that power from God's Word. If you are a Christian, the following three things are true about you:

1. *God has Given You His Indwelling Spirit.*

Before Jesus was crucified and risen from the dead, He made a wonderful promise to His disciples.

> *"And I will ask the Father, and he will give you another Counselor to be with you forever-- the Spirit of truth. The world cannot accept him, because it neither sees him nor knows him. But you know him, for <u>he lives with you and will be in you</u>."* – John 14:16-17

Prior to Jesus' ascension into heaven the Holy Spirit worked with His disciples, but Jesus said there was coming a time when the Spirit would be "in" those who are Christians. Just before Jesus left the earth He gave this promise:

> *"But <u>you will receive power</u> when the Holy Spirit comes on you; and you will be my witnesses in Jerusalem, and in all Judea and Samaria, and to the ends of the earth."* – Acts 1:8

And on the Day of Pentecost, after having received this gift of the Holy Spirit, Peter got up and preached a sermon where this Spirit was promised to others:

> *"Repent and be baptized, every one of you, in the name of Jesus Christ for the forgiveness of your sins. And <u>you will receive the gift of the Holy Spirit</u>."* – Acts 2:38

And of course, the "gift of the Holy Spirit" is the Holy Spirit Himself. In other words, God Himself has promised to literally indwell those who place their trust in Jesus Christ as Savior and Lord.

> *Don't you realize that all of you together are the temple of God and that <u>the Spirit of God lives in you</u>? God will bring ruin upon anyone who ruins this temple. For God's temple is holy, and <u>you Christians are that temple</u>.* – 1 Corinthians 3:16-17

Now the reason this is so important is because you and I need to know that God is fully and completely available to us 24/7. And the reason we know this is because He is with us, in us, literally living within us right now, at this very moment. You do not need to go searching for God, because God is within you.

Now notice that I didn't say that you are God, because you're not, but God the Holy Spirit has taken up residence in your body. Everywhere that you go, God goes with you – everything that you say, God hears – every action that you take, you are inviting God to join you in it. The power of God is available to you, because God is literally here, present, with us each and every moment of our lives.

2. God has Given You Spiritual Power.

Erwin McManus, in "Seizing Your Divine Moment" tells about his son, Aaron. "One summer Aaron went to a youth camp. He was just a little guy, and I was kind of glad because it was a church camp. I figured he wasn't going to hear all those ghost stories, because ghost stories can really cause a kid to have nightmares. But unfortunately, since it was a Christian camp and they didn't tell ghost stories, because we don't believe in ghosts, they told demon and Satan stories instead. And so when Aaron got home, he was terrified. 'Dad, don't turn off the light!' he said before going to bed. 'No, Daddy, could you stay here with me? Daddy, I'm afraid. They told all these stories about demons.' And I wanted to say, 'They're not real.' He goes, 'Daddy, Daddy, would you pray for me that I would be safe?' I could feel it – I could feel warm-blanket Christianity beginning to wrap around him, a life of safety, safety, safety. I said, 'Aaron, I will not pray for you to be safe. I will pray that God will make you dangerous, so dangerous that demons will flee when you enter the room.' And he goes, 'All right. But pray I would be really, really dangerous, Daddy.'

Isn't that the kind of prayer we should be praying? That in God's power we would live lives that would make demons tremble? While it is great to know we are safe in God's arms, it's just as important to know that God has empowered us to be spiritually dangerous to the opposition. We need to understand that with God literally living within us, and by having a gift supernaturally given to us by God, that we have the power to become everything God's wants us to become, and that makes us spiritually dangerous to our enemy. But that kind of power does not come by approaching God from a position of strength, but rather, from one of surrender.

Do not get drunk on wine, which leads to debauchery. Instead, be filled with the Spirit. Speak to one another with psalms, hymns and spiritual songs. Sing and make music in your heart to the Lord. – Ephesians 5:18-19

Just as alcohol can control you in a negative way, the Holy Spirit can control you in the most positive way imaginable, but only when we surrender our lives to Him. And when we surrender our lives to Him, He promises us fullness of power. That surrender involves a putting away of sin, of repenting of things that are displeasing to God, and living a life of obedience.

But if Christ is in you, your body is dead because of sin, yet your spirit is alive because of righteousness. And if the Spirit of him who raised Jesus from the dead is living in you, he who raised Christ from the dead will also give life to your mortal bodies through his Spirit, who lives in you. – Romans 8:10-11

God promises us the same type of power that was used to raise Jesus from the dead. It is the power that allows us to live holy lives. It is the power that gives us the strength for the journey, Ut is the power that gives us the boldness to tell others about our faith in Christ, It is the power that grants us victory in spiritual warfare. This is the kind of power that you and I need to live the type of lives that are pleasing, satisfactory, sufficient, and dedicated to God.

Early in the history of the church, the church had come under persecution, so they gathered together to pray to God, and look what happened:

After they prayed, the place where they were meeting was shaken. And they were all filled with the Holy Spirit and spoke the word of God boldly. – Acts 4:31

Notice that they were "filled" with the Holy Spirit. That only happens when we first empty ourselves of ourselves, and we replace our selfish desires with God's. And when we are filled with the Spirit, we will begin to see some phenomenal things beginning to take place in both our lives and the life of the church.

3. *God has Given You A Spiritual Gift.*

[1]Max DePree, CEO of Herman Miller, Inc., describes a simple, but profound, incident that altered the culture of his organization:

"In the furniture industry of the 1920's, the machines of most factories were not run by electric motors but by pulleys from a central drive shaft. The millwright was the person on whom the entire activity of the operation depended – He was the key person. One day, the millwright died. My father, being a young manager at the time, did not know what to do when a key person died, but thought he ought to go visit the family. He went to the house and was invited to join the family in the living room. The widow asked my father if it would be all right if she read aloud some poetry. Naturally, he agreed. She went into another room, came back with a bound book, and for many minutes read selected pieces of beautiful poetry. When she finished, my father commented on how beautiful the poetry was and asked who wrote it. She replied that her husband, the millwright, was the poet. It is now nearly 60 years since the millwright died, and my father and many of us at Herman Miller continue to wonder: Was he a poet who did millwright's work, or was he a millwright who wrote poetry?

Is that not how it is in the church? We have factory workers who are teachers, computer people who are elders, homemakers that work with the youth, and so on. The beautiful thing about having God's Spirit inside you is that He not only gives you the gift of Himself, but He supernaturally empowers you by giving you a spiritual gift you did not have before you became a Christian.

---

[1] Peter Grazier in "Work and Spirituality" on teambuildinginc.com; reprinted in Homiletics (September 2001), pp.13-14

We are not talking here about a natural talent, but about God giving you a gift to do something for His glory in the church; something that you did not have the ability to do before.

There are different kinds of gifts, but the same Spirit. There are different kinds of service, but the same Lord. There are different kinds of working, but the same God works all of them in all men. Now to each one the manifestation of the Spirit is given for the common good. – 1 Corinthians 12:4-7

Now I want you to notice that you are specifically given this spiritual gift as a means to assist the church. There are various lists of ministry gifts that we find in the New Testament, including leadership, hospitality, faith, giving, and so on – and I don't believe these lists are exhaustive. But what is necessary for us to do is to discover what our particular gift is and begin using it for ministry.

Each one should use whatever gift he has received to serve others, faithfully administering God's grace in its various forms. – 1 Peter 4:10

The four major lists of spiritual gifts are found in Romans 12:3-8, 1 Corinthians 12:1-11,27-31, Ephesians 4:11-12, and 1 Peter 4:9-11 but there are other passages that mention or illustrate gifts not included in these lists. All gifts are given to help the church fulfill its purposes.

You can discover and implement your spiritual gift in several ways:

1) Pray.

Such an undertaking must begin in prayer. As we have discussed in previous chapters, we must seek the will of our Heavenly Father. Pray that He would make it clear to you which gift He has given to you and how He desires for you to apply it.

2) Begin to ask your friends and family members what they believe God has gifted you to do.

Ask Christian friends and family members to point out areas where they think you are the strongest in ministering in God's Kingdom. Ask them to specifically list thing that they have noticed you are good at that perhaps you were not good at before you became a Christian.

3) Take a Spiritual Gifts Inventory.

There are a number of different spiritual gifts inventories that are available. Many of them ask you to go through a list of questions and grade yourself to see where it is most likely that God has gifted you. While I would be hesitant to only base my knowledge of my spiritual gift(s) on an inventory, it can be a helpful exercise to get you started in the right direction.

4) Start using your spiritual gift in the church and in other situations.

Once you have some idea of what your spiritual gift is, start ministering in that area of the church and see if it is a good fit. God wants you to lead a fulfilling, spiritually successful, and powerful life, but that will not reach its fruition until you begin using the gift He has given to you. Many people are dissatisfied because they find themselves working in areas that they are not gifted in. When your gift matches your "job description" you will find fulfillment like you've never experienced before.

CHAPTER 16: THE WORK OF THE HOLY SPIRIT IN PROPHETS AND APOSTLES

1. *The work of the Holy Spirit in apostles and prophets is an entirely distinctive work. He imparts to apostles and prophets a special gift for a special purpose.*

> *There are different kinds of gifts, but the same Spirit. –* 1 Corinthians 12:4

> *To one there is given through the Spirit the message of wisdom, to another the message of knowledge by means of the same Spirit, to another faith by the same Spirit, to another gifts of healing by that one Spirit, to another miraculous powers, <u>to another prophecy</u>, to another distinguishing between spirits, to another speaking in different kinds of tongues, and to still another the interpretation of tongues. All these are the work of one and the same Spirit, and he gives them to each one, just as he determines. –* 1 Corinthians 12:8-11

> *And in the church God has appointed <u>first of all apostles</u>, <u>second prophets</u>, third teachers, then workers of miracles, also those having gifts of healing, those able to help others, those with gifts of administration, and those speaking in different kinds of tongues. <u>Are all apostles?</u> <u>Are all prophets?</u> Are all teachers? Do all work miracles? –* 1 Corinthians 12:28-29

It is evident from these verses that the work of the Holy Spirit in apostles and prophets is of a distinctive character. The doctrine is becoming very common and very popular in our day that the work of the Holy Spirit in preachers and teachers and in ordinary believers, illuminating them and guiding them into the truth and opening their minds to understand the Word of God is the same in kind and differs only in degree from the work of the Holy Spirit in prophets and apostles. It is evident from the passage just cited that this doctrine is thoroughly unscriptural and untrue. It overlooks the fact so clearly stated and carefully elucidated that while there is "the same Spirit" there are "different kinds of gifts" and that not all are prophets and not all are apostles. There is much reasoning in these days about inspiration that appears at first sight very learned, but that will not bear much rigid scrutiny or candid comparison with the exact statements of the Word of God.

2. *Truth hidden from man for ages and which they had not discovered and could not discover by the unaided processes of human reasoning has been revealed to apostles and prophets in the Spirit.*

> *That is, the mystery made known to me <u>by revelation</u>, as I have already written briefly. In reading this, then, you will be able to understand my insight into the mystery of Christ, which was not made known to men in other generations as <u>it has now been revealed by the Spirit to God's holy apostles and prophets</u>.* – Ephesians 3:3-5

The Bible contains truth that men had never discovered before the Bible stated it. It contains truth that men never could have discovered if left to themselves. Our heavenly Father, in great grace, has revealed this truth to us His children THROUGH His servants, THE APOSTLES AND THE PROPHETS. The Holy Spirit is the agent of this revelation. There are many who tell us today that we should test the statements of Scripture by the conclusions of human reasoning. The folly of this is evident when we bear in mind that the revelation of God transcends human reasoning, and that any consciousness that is not the product of the study and absorption of Bible truth is not really a Christian consciousness. The fact that the Bible does contain truth that man had never discovered we know not merely because it is stated in the Scriptures, but we know it also as a matter of fact. There is not one of the most distinctive and precious doctrines taught in the Bible that men have ever discovered apart from the Bible. If our consciousness differs from the statements of this Book, which is so plainly God's Book, it is not yet fully Christian and the thing we do not want to do is to try to pull God's revelation down to the level of our consciousness but to lift our consciousness up to the level of God's Word.

3. *The revelation made to the prophets was independent of their own thinking. It was made to them by the Spirit of Christ which was in them. And was a subject of inquiry to their own mind as to its meaning. It was not their own thought, but His.*

Concerning this salvation, the prophets, who spoke of the grace that was to come to you, <u>searched intently and with the greatest care, trying to find out the time and circumstances to which the Spirit of Christ in them was pointing</u> when he predicted the sufferings of Christ and the glories that would follow. <u>It was revealed to them</u> that they were not serving themselves but you, when they spoke of the things that have now been told you by those who have preached the gospel to you <u>by the Holy Spirit</u> sent from heaven. Even angels long to look into these things. – 1 Peter 1:10-12

These words make it plain that a Person in the prophets, and independent of the prophets – the Holy Spirit – revealed truth which was independent of their own thinking, which they did not altogether understand themselves, and regarding which it was necessary that they make diligent search and study. Another Person than themselves was thinking and speaking and they were seeking to comprehend what He said.

4. *No prophet's utterance was of the prophet's own will, but he spoke from God, and the prophet was carried along in his utterance by the Holy Spirit.*

For prophecy never had its origin in the will of man, but men spoke from God as <u>they were carried along by the Holy Spirit</u>. – 2 Peter 1:21

Clearly then, the prophet was simply an instrument in the hands of another, as the Spirit of God carried him along, so he spoke.

5. *It was the Holy Spirit who spoke in the prophetic utterances. It was His word that was upon the prophet's tongue.*

So, <u>as the Holy Spirit says</u>: "Today, if you hear his voice... – Hebrews 3:7

<u>The Holy Spirit also testifies</u> to us about this. First <u>he says</u>: "This is the covenant I will make with them after that time, says the Lord. I will put my laws in their hearts, and I will write them on their minds." – Hebrews 10:15-16

They disagreed among themselves and began to leave after Paul had made this final statement: "The Holy Spirit spoke the truth to your forefathers when he said through Isaiah the prophet: – Acts 28:25

"The Spirit of the LORD spoke through me; his word was on my tongue. – 2 Samuel 23:2

Over and over again in these passages we are told that it was the Holy Spirit who was the speaker in the prophetic utterances and that it was His word, not theirs, that was upon the prophet's tongue. The prophet was simply the mouth by which the Holy Spirit spoke. As a man, that is except as the Spirit taught him and used him, the prophet might be as fallible as other men are but when the Spirit was upon him and he was taken up and carried along by the Holy Spirit, he was infallible in his teachings; for his teachings in that case were not his own, but the teachings of the Holy Spirit. When carried along by the Holy Spirit it was God who was speaking and not the prophet. For example, there can be little doubt that Paul had many mistaken notions about many things but when he taught as an Apostle in the Spirit's power, he was infallible—or rather the Spirit, who taught through him was infallible and the consequent teaching was infallible—as infallible as God Himself. We do well to carefully distinguish what Paul may have thought as a man and what he actually did teach as an Apostle. In the Bible we have the record of what he taught as an Apostle. There are those who think that in 1 Corinthians 7:6, 25 that Paul admits that he was not sure in this case that he had the word of the Lord.

I say this as a concession, not as a command. – 1 Corinthians 7:6

Now about virgins: I have no command from the Lord, but I give a judgment as one who by the Lord's mercy is trustworthy. – 1 Corinthians 7:25

If Paul was not speaking on the Lord's behalf in this passage (which is more than doubtful) we see how careful he was when he was not sure to note the fact and this gives us additional certainty in all other passages. It is sometimes said that Paul taught in his early ministry that the Lord would return during his lifetime, and that in this he was, of course, mistaken. But Paul never taught anywhere that the

Lord would return in his lifetime. It is true he says in 1 Thessalonians 4:17:

> After that, <u>we who are still alive</u> and are left will be caught up together with them in the clouds to meet the Lord in the air. And so we will be with the Lord forever. – 1 Thessalonians 4:17

As he was still living when he wrote the words, he naturally and properly did not include himself with those who had already fallen asleep in speaking of the Lord's return. But this is not to assert that he would remain alive until the Lord came. Quite probably at this period of his ministry he entertained the hope that he might remain alive and consequently lived in an attitude of expectancy, but the attitude of expectancy is the true attitude in all ages for each believer. It is quite probable that Paul expected that he would be alive until the coming of the Lord, but if he did expect this, he did not teach it. The Holy Spirit kept him from this as from all other errors in his teachings.

6. *The Holy Spirit in the Apostle taught not only the thought (or "concept") but the words in which the thought was to he expressed.*

> This is what we speak, <u>not in words</u> taught us by human wisdom <u>but in words taught by the Spirit</u>, expressing spiritual truths in spiritual words. – 1 Corinthians 2:13

This passage clearly teaches that the words, as well as the thought, were chosen and taught by the Holy Spirit. This is also a necessary inference from the fact that thought is conveyed from mind to mind by words and it is the words which express the thought, and if the words were imperfect, the thought expressed in these words would necessarily be imperfect and to that extent be untrue. Nothing could be plainer than Paul's statement "IN WORDS taught by the Spirit." The Holy Spirit has Himself anticipated all the modern ingenious and wholly unbiblical and false theories regarding His own work in the Apostles. The more carefully and minutely we study THE WORDING of the statements of this wonderful Book, the more we will become convinced of the marvellous accuracy of the words used to express the thought. Very often the solution of an apparent difficulty is found in studying the exact words used. The accuracy, precision and inerrancy of the exact words used is amazing. To the superficial student, the doctrine of verbal inspiration may appear questionable or even absurd; any regenerated and Spirit-taught man, who PONDERS THE WORDS of the Scripture day after day and year after year, will become convinced that the wisdom of God is in the very words, as well as in the thought which the words endeavor to convey. A change of a word, or letter, or a tense, or case, or number, in many instances would land us into contradiction or untruth, but taking THE WORDS EXACTLY as written, difficulties disappear and truth shines forth. The Divine origin of nature shines forth more clearly in the use of a microscope as we see the perfection of form and adaptation of means to end of the minutest particles of matter. In a similar manner, the Divine origin of the Bible shines forth more clearly under the microscope as we notice the perfection with which the turn of a word reveals the absolute thought of God.

But someone may ask, "If the Holy Spirit is the author of the words of Scripture, how do we account for variations in style and diction? How do we explain for instance that Paul always used Pauline language and John Johannine language, etc.?" The answer to this is very simple. If we could not account at all for this fact, it would have but little weight against the explicit statement of God's Word with any one who is humble enough and wise enough to recognize that there are a great many things which he cannot account for at all which could be easily accounted for if he knew more. But these variations are easily accounted for. The Holy Spirit is quite wise enough and has quite enough ability in the use of language in revealing truth to and through any given individual, to use words, phrases and forms of expression and idioms in that person's vocabulary and forms of thought, and to make use of that person's peculiar individuality. Indeed, it is a mark of the Divine wisdom of this Book that the same truth is expressed with absolute accuracy in such widely variant forms of expression.

7. *The utterances of the Apostles and the prophets were the Word of God. When we read these words, we are listening not to the voice of man, but to the voice of God.*

"Thus you nullify <u>the word of God</u> by your tradition that you have handed down. And you do many things like that." – Mark 7:13

Jesus had been setting the law given through Moses over against the Pharisaic traditions, and in doing this, He expressly says in this passage that the law given through Moses was "THE WORD OF GOD."

"The Spirit of the LORD spoke through me; <u>his word</u> was on my tongue. – 2 Samuel 23:2

Here again we are told that the utterance of God's prophet was the word of God. In a similar way God says:

And we also thank God continually because, when <u>you received the word of God, which you heard from us</u>, you accepted it not as the word of men, but as it actually is, <u>the word of God</u>, which is at work in you who believe. – 1 Thessalonians 2:13

Here Paul declares that the word which he spoke, taught by the Spirit of God, was THE WORD OF GOD.

CHAPTER 17: THE WORK OF THE HOLY SPIRIT IN JESUS CHRIST

Jesus Christ Himself is the one perfect manifestation in history of the complete work of the Holy Spirit in man.

1. *Jesus Christ was begotten of the Holy Spirit.*

> *The angel answered, "The Holy Spirit will come upon you, and the power of the Most High will overshadow you. So the holy one to be born will be called the Son of God. –* Luke 1:35

As we have already seen, in regeneration the believer is begotten of God, but Jesus Christ was begotten of God in His original generation. He is the only begotten Son of God (John 3:16). It was entirely by the Spirit's power working in Mary that the Son of God was formed within her. The regenerated man has a carnal nature received from his earthly father and a new nature imparted by God. Jesus Christ had only the one holy nature, that which in man is called the new nature. Nevertheless, He was a real man as He had a human mother.

2. *Jesus Christ led a holy and spotless life and offered Himself unblemished to God through the working of the Holy Spirit.*

> *How much more, then, will the blood of Christ, <u>who through the eternal Spirit offered himself unblemished to God</u>, cleanse our consciences from acts that lead to death, so that we may serve the living God! –* Hebrews 9:14

Jesus Christ met and overcame temptations as other men may meet and overcome them, in the power of the Holy Spirit. He was tempted and suffered through temptation (Hebrews 3:18), He was tempted in all points like as we are (Hebrews 4:15), but never once in any way did He yield to temptation. He was tempted entirely apart from sin (Hebrews 4:15), but He won His victories in a way that is open for all of us to win victory, in the power of the Holy Spirit.

3. *Jesus Christ was anointed and fitted for service by the Holy Spirit.*

God anointed Jesus of Nazareth <u>with the Holy Spirit and</u> <u>power</u>, and how he went around doing good and healing all who were under the power of the devil, because God was with him. – Acts 10:38

In a prophetic vision of the coming Messiah in the Old Testament we read:

<u>The Spirit of the Sovereign LORD is on me</u>, because the LORD has anointed me to preach good news to the poor. He has sent me to bind up the brokenhearted, to proclaim freedom for the captives and release from darkness for the prisoners – Isaiah 61:1

In Luke's record of the earthly life of our Lord we read:

Jesus returned to Galilee <u>in the power of the Spirit</u>, and news about him spread through the whole countryside. – Luke 4:14

In a similar way Jesus said of Himself when speaking in the synagogue in Nazareth:

"<u>The Spirit</u> of the Lord is on me, because he has anointed me to preach good news to the poor. He has sent me to proclaim freedom for the prisoners and recovery of sight for the blind, to release the oppressed, to proclaim the year of the Lord's favor." – Luke 4:18-19

All these passages contain the one lesson, that it was by the special anointing with the Holy Spirit that Jesus Christ was qualified for the service to which God had called Him. As He stood in the Jordan after His baptism:

The Spirit of God descending like a dove and lighting on him... – Matthew 3:16b

It was then and there that He was anointed with the Holy Spirit and equipped for the service that lay before Him. Jesus Christ received His equipment for service in the same way that we receive ours by a definite anointing with the Holy Spirit.

4. *Jesus Christ was led by the Holy Spirit in His movements here upon earth.*

Jesus, full of the Holy Spirit, returned from the Jordan and was led by the Spirit in the desert. – Luke 4:1

Living as a man here upon earth and setting an example for us, each step of His life was under the Holy Spirit's guidance.

5. *Jesus Christ was taught by the Spirit who rested upon Him. The Spirit of God was the source of His wisdom in the days of His flesh.*

In the Old Testament prophecy of the coming Messiah we read:

The Spirit of the LORD will rest on him--the Spirit of wisdom and of understanding, the Spirit of counsel and of power, the Spirit of knowledge and of the fear of the LORD--and he will delight in the fear of the LORD. He will not judge by what he sees with his eyes, or decide by what he hears with his ears. – Isaiah 11:2-3

"Here is my servant, whom I uphold, my chosen one in whom I delight; I will put my Spirit on him and he will bring justice to the nations." – Isaiah 42:1

Matthew tells us (Matthew 12:17-18) that this prophecy was fulfilled in Jesus of Nazareth.

6. *The Holy Spirit abode upon Jesus in all His fullness and the words He spoke in consequence were the very words of God.*

For the one whom God has sent speaks the words of God, for God gives the Spirit without limit. – John 3:34

7. *After His resurrection, Jesus Christ gave instructions to His Apostles whom He had chosen through the Holy Spirit.*

In my former book, Theophilus, I wrote about all that Jesus began to do and to teach until the day he was taken up to heaven, after giving instructions through the Holy Spirit to the apostles he had chosen. – Acts 1:1-3

This relates to the time after His resurrection and so we see Jesus still working in the power of the Holy Spirit even *after* His resurrection from the dead.

8. *Jesus Christ performed His miracles here on earth in the power of the Holy Spirit.*

"I drive out demons by the Spirit of God..." – Matthew 12:28a

It is through the Spirit that miracle working power was given to some in the church after our Lord's departure from this earth (1 Corinthians 12:9-10), and in the power of the same Spirit, Jesus Christ wrought His miracles.

9. *It was by the power of the Holy Spirit that Jesus Christ was raised from the dead.*

And if the Spirit of him who raised Jesus from the dead is living in you, he who raised Christ from the dead will also give life to your mortal bodies through his Spirit, who lives in you. – Romans 8:11

The same Spirit who is to awaken our mortal bodies and is going to raise us up in some future day raised up Jesus.

Several things are plainly evident from this study of the work of the Holy Spirit in Jesus Christ:

First of all, we see the completeness of His humanity. He lived and He thought, He worked, He taught, He conquered sin and won victories for God in the power of that very same Spirit whom it is our privilege also to have.

In the second place, we see our own utter dependence upon the Holy Spirit. If it was in the power of the Holy Spirit that Jesus Christ, the only begotten Son of God, lived and worked, achieved and triumphed, how much more dependent are we upon Him at every turn of life and in every phase of service and every experience of conflict with Satan and sin.

The third thing that is evident is the wondrous world of privilege, blessing and victory and conquest that is open to us. The same Spirit by which Jesus was originally begotten, is at our disposal for us to be begotten again of Him. The same Spirit by which Jesus offered Himself without spot to God is at our disposal that we also may offer ourselves without spot to Him. The same Spirit by which Jesus was anointed for service is at our disposal that we may be anointed for service. The same Spirit who led Jesus Christ in His movements here on earth is ready to lead us today. The same Spirit who taught Jesus and imparted to Him wisdom and understanding, counsel and might, and knowledge and the fear of the Lord is here to teach us. Jesus Christ is our pattern (1 John 2:6), "the first born among many brothers" (Romans 8:29). Whatever He realized through the Holy Spirit is for us to realize also today.

THANK YOU FOR INVESTING IN THIS BOOK!

We'd love to hear your feedback. Please stop by and leave a review at: **http://www.amazon.com/author/barrydavis** . You can also check out our other books there.

If you'd like to see some of our many resources for Bible Study leaders and Pastors, please go to:
http://www.pastorshelper.com

I hope to hear from you soon! May God bless you as you continue to serve Him.

In Christ,

Barry L. Davis

Printed in Great Britain
by Amazon